Tales from a Clubroom

Co-authors Bernard Bragg *seated on stool* and Eugene Bergman *seated on dais* address the cast in rehearsal.

TALES FROM A CLUBROOM

Bernard Bragg   Eugene Bergman

with a foreword by McCay Vernon

Gallaudet College Press
Washington, D.C.

Published by Gallaudet College Press
Kendall Green, Washington, D.C. 20002

ISBN Number 0-913580-73-2
Library of Congress Catalogue Card Number 81-81925

Frontispiece photograph by William L. Klender. All other photographs by Charles Shoup.

Jacket illustration by Claire Bergman.

Gallaudet College is an equal opportunity employer/educational institution. Programs and services offered by Gallaudet College receive substantial financial support from the U.S. Department of Education.

To the late
Frederick Hughes
and to
Wolf Bragg,
Fathers of American Deaf Theatre.

In any city, the club of the deaf is the heart of the deaf community. It is the principal meeting place and forum of the deaf. It is, in most cases, the only place where they can socialize. It is their ballroom, their bar, their motion picture house, their theatre, their coffeehouse, their community center—all rolled into one. It is a piece of their own land in exile—an oasis in the world of sound.

FOREWORD

Playwrights Bragg and Bergman have taken the deaf club as the setting for a brilliant play in which they capture in dramatic form the psychological impact of deafness on human beings. Just as the novelist Sinclair Lewis portrayed the essence of Americana using the ubiquitous Rotary Club as the focal point of middle America's social life, so have Bragg and Bergman given us a penetrating and fascinating view of Deaf America through the vehicle of the deaf club in *Tales from a Clubroom*. Their characters capture the essence of deafness as a human condition just as Babbitt, Lowell Schmaltz, and other literary figures of Sinclair Lewis' novels epitomized the life of his era.

A club offers its members an opportunity for human intimacy, with all its potential for love-hate relationships. The alternative to this intimacy is isolation. It is this human dilemma, and the resultant love-hate relationships, that are powerfully and intricately woven in *Tales from a Clubroom*. One sees the deaf peddler demeaned for the beggar image he creates, but admired as a symbol of revenge wrought upon "hearies" for their exploitation of deaf people. The arrogant, insensitive college student; the oft married aging *femme fatale;* the frustrated actress who directs the club's skits; the amiable, outgoing club man who operates the movie projector; the oralist emerging from his closet; the socially inadequate "hearie" who clings to the deaf—all of the "main players" in almost any club for the deaf in any city of the United States are powerfully portrayed.

As the play begins, those not closely identified with the deaf community will feel somewhat lost, just as a non-Jew might feel viewing a Yiddish drama. However, the story told in *Tales from a Clubroom* has a generality for all people.

McCay Vernon

A WORD FROM THE AUTHORS . . .

A TEXT WITHOUT ANY EMBELLISHMENT

The viewer of a subtitled foreign movie pays only the barest attention to the subtitles as they flash on the screen. He or she is so completely caught up in the emotions and insights radiated by the movements and expressions of the actors—if the movie is any good—that he or she resorts to reading the subtitles only as a prop in order to understand better what is going on.

The script of *Tales from a Clubroom* was conceived in nearly the same spirit. In a normal play, dialogue is the flesh and bones while action is the spirit. But *Tales from a Clubroom* is not a normal play: its dialogue, at least in the English-language version, provides the bare bones only. Our script provides "English subtitles" for a play that must be *seen* in the plumage of another language—American Sign Language (ASL)—in order to be appreciated.

This is not to detract from the value of the script. Written English can be used to convey to some extent the richness, vitality, and dramatic impact of ASL as used by the actors. The translation, however, then would not be faithful. The structure of ASL is so radically different from that of English that our ASL dialogue abounds in untranslatable puns and nuances of feeling which cannot be approximated by English idioms and slang expressions without making the play a travesty of itself. We did not want our slice of life to be chopped into hash.

We were thus left with two other options for conveying the flavor of the play—the flavor of what the deaf are like among themselves. One option was to translate literally into English every sign used in the play. We decided against this approach, since we did not want to write our script in some sort of pidgin English, of the kind used by American movie makers to suggest South Sea Islanders ("Me go home." "You belong him. . . . "). That would tax the reader's patience and distort the play as in a funhouse mirror. So ultimately we decided to write our script in the plainest and barest English possible, while at the same time reflecting the rhythm of ASL. Our decision was partially prompted by the belief that this text will also be used by theatrical companies of the deaf nationwide: we wanted to stimulate their inventiveness in improvising the best and most expressive signs on the basis of a relatively neutral English dialogue that would not confuse them by idioms and expressions foreign to ASL.

There is a saying that you can judge a good Chinese restaurant by the number of Chinese who frequent it. It is a fact and not puffery that this play, written by the deaf for the deaf, has met with enthusiastic responses from deaf audiences wherever it was performed. So there must be something genuine about it—something with which the deaf can identify—and that was our aim in the first place. Since the play seems genuine, perhaps it can provide the hearing with a bridge to the deaf world, a bridge from which one can catch a glimpse of the subterranean world of the deaf— that glowing and colorful world in which ordinary and even banal emotions are heightened into drama through the medium of sign language. This, then, is the principal reason why we offer a printed version of the play, a version written in sparse and terse language conveying the rhythm of ASL better than a fluent and idiomatic English version that would, in our opinion, smother the living spirit of the play.

Deaf audiences laugh uproariously and often when they see our play. Bitterness and black humor usually do not produce this kind of response. The laughter of our audiences is healthy. As we see it, and as we know other deaf people see it, our play reflects the vibrant and buoyant life of a close-knit community. A cruel community would not be so ready to forgive a member such as the arrogant college graduate who, after defying it, admits his mistake. A cruel community would not show the tolerance and compassion for life's unfortunates that the members of the Metro Club of the Deaf display toward Spivey, the pariah, and Ballin, the vision-impaired young deaf man. As Greene, the Club's president, puts it, "We look out for each other! . . . We're sincere. We really care for each other. . . . We have hearts!" And there is nothing banal about that vigorous spirit of our club members. Even their gossip resonates with an elemental vitality. When they complain of the misery they endure in a hearing-dominated world that they never made, their complaints are not bitter and hateful but expressed in the form of rollicking Rabelaisian jokes or in a life-affirming spirit.

Deaf audiences who saw our play in cities as widely disparate as Cincinnati, Washington, D.C., New York, and Boston, have commented on the familiarity of characters and the club setting. It seems that most clubs for the deaf in the United States have the same setting of a bar with stools, a jukebox, a dais, trophies on the walls, and tables with chairs. As for familiar characters, Lawrence Newman's review of *Tales* in *The Deaf American* of October, 1980, explores this aspect in some depth.

One unexpected result was that, in the months following the premiere of *Tales* in Cincinnati in June, 1980, treasurers in several clubs of the deaf across the nation were found to have embezzled club treasuries and were expelled. Life imitates art, eh?

One final note: People like Spivey, the pariah, do exist and are encountered in more than a few clubs of the deaf. Following each performance of the play, deaf spectators commented to us that Spivey's behavior bears an uncanny resemblance to individuals whom they met in their local clubs. "Isolattoes" (as Melville calls them), such as Spivey, locked in the rigor of noögenic paresis, stand in stark contrast to the vigorous, robust, and gregarious deaf majority. They are very few, but they do exist, as if to point up the unusual extremes met with among the deaf. But then extremes are natural among a unique and intriguing minority whom the invisible handicap of deafness has placed in an extreme existential situation.

Bernard Bragg
Eugene Bergman

ACKNOWLEDGEMENTS

We are indebted to the following people for comments and suggestions: Eric Malzkuhn, Simon Carmel, Cathy Kalbacher, Kathleen Callaway, and Elaine Costello.

We also are deeply grateful to the original cast of *Tales from a Clubroom,* whose personal reactions during rehearsals contributed to much of the play's intended realism.

Our thanks also go the the late Fred Schreiber and to Gary Olsen for their faith in us and for commissioning our play, sight unseen.

Tales from a Clubroom was first staged by the Hughes Memorial Theatre/Model Community Theatre of the Deaf with the sponsorship of the National Association of the Deaf, the Kellogg Special School of the Future, the National Committee: Arts for the Handicapped, and the Division of Public Services of Gallaudet College. The premier performance at the Palace Theatre in Cincinnati, Ohio, highlighted the Centennial Convention of the National Association of the Deaf, July 1-3, 1980.

The original cast included:

SHIRLEY KLAYMANS	Eileen Bechara
WILL GRADY	Larry Berke
KATHY GREENE	Lilly Berke
GARY MCALLISTER	Steve Brunelle
TIM SHALLECK	Charles Buemi
JAY MACHER	Frank Del Rosso
JIM YAKUBSKI	Robert Dillman
MARY BRANNON	Georgetta Doran
MARK LINDSEY	William Ennis
SPENCER COLLINS	Thomas Fields
WINONA SHOEMAKER	Elizabeth Hathaway
ABE GREENE	Thomas Janulewicz
WILLIE FUTRELL	Jerry Jones, Jr.
EVELYN JACKSON	Cathy Kalbacher
ALAN BALLIN	Stephen Kimble
THOMAS SPIVEY	Jerry Little
CHARLES CARSWELL	Richard K. Moore
JEAN FUTRELL	Adele Shuart
JANICE WISEMAN	Nancy Torbett
IDA YAKUBSKI	Sarah Val

Directed by Bernard Bragg
Sets Created by Mickey Fields and Louis Val
Lighting and Stage Management by John Johnston
Stage Manager Assisted by Alan Matthews

Technical Assistant Glenna Garner
Costume Mistress Wanda Berke
Assistants to the Director Janet DeLap and Hortense Auerbach

Tales from a Clubroom

CHARACTERS

JIM YAKUBSKI
Club treasurer, peacemaker, legal counselor.

IDA YAKUBSKI
His wife, a motherly lady who is responsible for coffee and sandwiches.

ABE GREENE
Club president; uses salty language and has a domineering manner; always chomping on a cigar.

KATHY GREENE
His wife, an excitable, lively woman; a drama fan, always on the go; thinks of skits as the most sophisticated form of drama.

MARK LINDSEY
Young graduate of Gallaudet College; signs "Englishy," that is, with English syntax.

SHIRLEY KLAYMANS
Thrice divorced blonde; shapely, fun-lover, laughs easily.

MARY BRANNON
Club deadbeat; a mannish young woman with a savage, furtive manner.

WILL GRADY
Operator of the club's movie projector; wears a suit and bow tie, unlike most others; laughs readily, the club's jokester.

TIM SHALLECK
Muscular bartender with limited education; he uses only the simplest and most picturesque signs (ASL[1]).

JANICE WISEMAN
Garrulous alcoholic widow.

WILLIE FUTRELL
TTY[2] repairman; an earnest man.

JEAN FUTRELL
His wife; a spitfire of a woman who loves to gossip.

CHARLES CARSWELL
ABC[3] (manual alphabet) card peddler; flashy dresser; self-assured.

WINONA SHOEMAKER
A young girl; a recent graduate of a school for the deaf.

GARY McALLISTER
Light on his feet, a basketball player.

JAY MACHER
Old-time basketball coach.

THOMAS SPIVEY
Club pariah; with a fixed grin on his face, he somehow manages to be near the focus of most conversations without ever saying anything himself.

EVELYN JACKSON
Hearing spinster; the daughter of deaf parents; feels comfortable with the deaf and likes to consort with them.

ALAN BALLIN
Naive young man with tunnel vision (Usher's Syndrome[4]).

SPENCER COLLINS
Young ex-oralist;[5] signs awkwardly.

SETTING

TIME

The present. Act One, a Saturday night in March; Act Two, later that same evening; Act Three, two weeks later than the opening. That is, the play starts and ends within a two-week period in early March.

PLACE

All action takes place at the Metro Club of the Deaf. The stage shows a large room dominated by an array of tables and chairs in the foreground and a dais and an oblong bar in the background. The room's walls are decorated with pictures of past presidents and members, an old CISS (Comité International des Sports des Sourds[6]) *poster, and shelves bearing basketball trophies and* Golden Lightnings *pennants. A jukebox occupies a prominent place to the right. During the film showings, a screen is placed on the dais.*

ACT ONE

A Saturday evening in March at the Metro Club of the Deaf. Darkness. Finale of a film being shown with titles rising on the screen, which the players face, seated so as to show three-fourths of their backs to the audience. Lights go on. Everybody starts talking at once.

MRS. GREENE
(Stands up.) Lights? Hurry up! Turn on the lights. Lights?

MACHER
(Waves at the projector light to attract GRADY'S attention and stands up. To EVERYONE.) That's the way he is. He's always asleep. He already saw the movie last night. (MACHER moves toward GRADY and shakes him awake.)

GRADY
(Hurries to work on the projector. To MACHER.) What did you flick my nose for?

MACHER
Because it's too long.

YAKUBSKI
(Climbs on the dais and hushes everybody up.) Ready for the door prizes! Stay seated. (To MRS. YAKUBSKI.) Get the box with tickets.

MRS. YAKUBSKI
(To GREENE.) Greene, where's the box?

GREENE
(To SHALLECK.) Box, over there. (Points behind the bar.) Bring it. (GREENE takes box from SHALLECK and carries it to MRS. YAKUBSKI.)

YAKUBSKI
Any volunteers? *(CARSWELL and then KLAYMANS rise, but YAK-UBSKI points at LINDSEY. CARSWELL and KLAYMANS return to their seats. To LINDSEY.)* Come, come!

LINDSEY
Me? *(Comes forward.)*

YAKUBSKI
Yes, you. *(To EVERYONE.)* This is Mark Lindsey. I am happy to introduce him to you. He graduated from Gallaudet College, Washington, D.C. He has moved to our city and is now a practice teacher at the school for the deaf. New blood. Welcome to our club, and have a good time!

LINDSEY
(To EVERYONE and YAKUBSKI.) Thank you. Happy to meet you all.

YAKUBSKI
Now please pick the winning ticket. Hold it! Remember, folks, I'll name only the last three digits on your tickets. *(Takes stub from LINDSEY.)* One, nine, eight, . . . one, nine, eight. . . . !

McALLISTER
Wow! Lookit! I won!

MACHER
Whoopee! *(Slaps McALLISTER on the back.)*

YAKUBSKI
Ah, here is the lucky winner of ten dollars. McAllister! Yesterday this guy tanked 37 points against the DAD.[7] You'd think he'd be satisfied? Nope—not him! Wants money, too. Well—OK, OK—but you better stay lucky till after the MSAD tournament. Don't let us down!

McALLISTER

I won't! I'll do my best. I promise you all to get another big trophy.
(**EVERYONE** *cheers.*)

YAKUBSKI

And now you draw the next ticket. (**McALLISTER** *plunges his hand
backward into the box, takes out a ticket, gives it to* **YAKUBSKI,**
then steps off the dais and through the seated crowd.)

YAKUBSKI

Second prize, eight dollars! One, two, five! One, two, five! I see
no takers. (*Pause.*) One, two, five!

GREENE

(*Peers at* **SPIVEY'S** *ticket; points at him.*) He won! (**SPIVEY** *is pro-
pelled gently by others toward the dais.*)

YAKUBSKI

Congratulations! This is the first time you've ever won a prize
here, right? (**SPIVEY** *nods slowly, in a daze.*) I'm sure you never
even won anything at bingo in church, either. Is that right? (**SPIVEY**
nods again.) You're lucky tonight! I'm happy you finally won the
jackpot. (**YAKUBSKI** *gives* **SPIVEY** *the money. Then* **SPIVEY** *is about
to return to his seat, but* **CARSWELL** *turns him around to return
him to the dais.* **CARSWELL** *sits down.*)

YAKUBSKI

(*To* **SPIVEY.**) Please select the next ticket. (**SPIVEY** *fumbles in box
as* **YAKUBSKI** *guides his hand.* **SPIVEY** *picks up several tickets,
putting them back in the box at* **YAKUBSKI'S** *behest, then picks out
one ticket and drops it on the floor.* **YAKUBSKI** *picks it up from the
floor. To* **EVERYONE.**) The third prize of five dollars goes to one,
one, two! One, one, two!

MRS. YAKUBSKI

(*Surprised, as she checks her ticket stub, she tries to catch* **YAKUBSKI'S** *attention and finally succeeds.)* I won! I won! *(She descends from dais to show her ticket to* MRS. FUTRELL *and* MRS. GREENE, *preens herself, and returns to the dais.* YAKUBSKI *gives her the money. She blows kisses at everyone and busses her husband on the cheek.)*

YAKUBSKI
Give it back to me! *(He takes the dollar bills from his wife's hand and stuffs them into his shirt pocket.)* Folks, believe me, I didn't do it on purpose. I didn't arrange for my wife to win. Guess I'm just naturally lucky to be married to a real winner. *(To* MRS. YAKUBSKI.*)* Now, my dear, pick out the next ticket. *(Notices* SPIVEY *still standing on the dais and patiently motions him to leave; he waits until* SPIVEY *sits down.)* Give it to me. The next prize is three bucks. The last prize. One, four, three! One, four, three!

KLAYMANS
One, four, three?

YAKUBSKI
Yes, one, four, three.

KLAYMANS
I won!

YAKUBSKI
Our lovely Klaymans. You always win a door prize. Do you use magic?

KLAYMANS
Guess I was born lucky.

YAKUBSKI
That's all. That was the last prize. *(*YAKUBSKI *gives the money to* KLAYMANS.*)*

(She puts it inside her blouse. CARSWELL *approaches and gestures as if he wants to snatch the money from her decolletage.* KLAYMANS *lightly swats away his hand and laughs.* BOTH *sit down.* MRS. YAKUBSKI *also sits down, taking the ticket box with her.)*

YAKUBSKI
(To EVERYONE.*)* Folks, before we have coffee, there are some important announcements. First, Macher has something to tell you. Where's Macher? Come.

MACHER
Everybody, look at me! Watch me! Saturday afternoon, March 18, in two weeks, is the final game of the MSAD tournament. I want all of you to come and support our club team, the "Golden Lightnings." *(*EVERYONE *cheers.)* Yes, we'll win the championship! All you club members come and show your strong support. Our team needs your support to keep up its spirits and win. We'll add one more big trophy to those shelves. *(*EVERYONE *continues to cheer.)*

YAKUBSKI
Thank you Macher. *(*MACHER *returns to his seat. To* MRS. GREENE.*)* You have an announcement?

MRS. GREENE
Don't forget, two weeks from now on the same Saturday, March 18, we will have our Far-out Skit Night. There will be many exciting and funny skits. Everyone come. Excuse my sign language! My children in school are influencing my signing; I'm using SEE.[8] Members, two dollars. Non-members, four dollars.

GREENE
(Moves toward the center of the stage, past EVERYONE'S *seats. To* MRS. GREENE.*)* I knew it. You forgot we are in THE . . . oops! . . . clubroom.

MRS. GREENE
See! You said "THE" in SEE. We're both doing it. *(EVERYONE laughs.)*

GREENE
Oh, forget it! *(Returns to his seat.)*

MRS. FUTRELL
(Stands up.) Saturday, March 18? But that's when the MAD club will hold its Movie Night. Won't there be a conflict?

MRS. GREENE
Who cares! If they want to hold their Movie Night then, that's their business. Nobody will go. Everyone will flock to our play. You all know that.

MRS. FUTRELL
Right! Nobody ever goes to that club anyway. It's so dull. All they do all the time is play poker, poker, poker. *(Sits down.)*

KLAYMANS
(Moves on the dais. To MRS. GREENE.) Non-members pay double, four dollars. Right?

MRS. GREENE
Right!

KLAYMANS
But what about my mother? Can't she pay less because she donated that stove to the club?

MRS. GREENE
Sorry, no exceptions. That's the club rule. Sorry!

KLAYMANS
I think that's a cheap thing to do after my mother helped the club so much. And now you want to charge her double. You're a bunch of cheapskates! Why should my mother join? She's hearing and very old and only comes here once or twice a year.

MRS. GREENE
No real problem. I guess our non-member label is meant to prevent deaf people who live around here from taking advantage of our hard work without paying any dues. How about two dollars for members and hearing people but four dollars for local deaf people?

KLAYMANS
That'll be fine.

GREENE
(Stands up on his chair. To MRS. GREENE *and* KLAYMANS.*)* Wait a minute . . . Wait a minute!

*(*SHALLECK *stands up, and taps* GREENE *on the leg.)*

SHALLECK
Don't stand on the chair. You're getting it dirty.

GREENE
(Ignores SHALLECK. *To* MRS. GREENE *and* KLAYMANS.*)* You can't make decisions like that, Kathy. You've got to wait until we have our next business meeting and submit a motion.

KLAYMANS
(To GREENE.*)* Why, Abe! I thought you loved me!

GREENE
Yes, I do. I always love you. But as President I have to run things the right way, don't I?

KLAYMANS

I feel hurt! *You* were the one crying and complaining because we couldn't afford a new stove when we first moved here.

GREENE

All right! I know, I know. Hell! I'll pay for your mother myself, half of that four dollars. Will that satisfy you?

KLAYMANS

(Snuggling up.) That's better. *(***KLAYMANS** *and* **MRS. GREENE** *return to their seats.)*

GREENE

(To **SHALLECK.***)* Well! What do you want?

SHALLECK

(To **GREENE.***)* Get off the chair.

YAKUBSKI

(To **SHALLECK.***)* Hold it! *(To the group.)* One more announcement. Our Board will meet the second Saturday from today, March 18, at seven. That's Skit Night. The meeting can't be postponed because the landlord wants to raise the rent again, and we'll have to discuss how to get the money.

FUTRELL

(Stands up.) I'm fed up. Let's move our club. *(Sits down.)*

MRS. FUTRELL

Right!

YAKUBSKI

People can't see you. Come here.

*(***FUTRELL** *steps onto the dais and repeats his opinion, facing the club members.)*

YAKUBSKI
That's easy for you to say. But where? Anyplace cheaper than this means it's less safe. The MAD club is in a worse neighborhood than ours, and its members have had their cars broken into.

MRS. WISEMAN
(Moves toward the platform. To EVERYONE.*)* This neighborhood isn't so safe either. Last week I saw some hoodlums hanging around the corner, and they started to follow me. Me . . . a poor lonely widow since my husband passed away a year ago. Did you all know that? I'm telling you, I'm getting scared to come here now.

GRADY
(Stands up behind the table where the movie projector is. To MRS. WISEMAN.*)* I'll drive you home tonight.

MRS. WISEMAN
How nice of you.

FUTRELL
Anyhow, we have enough money in the treasury to pay the added rent, don't we? I'm sure the club made a big profit from the Las Vegas Night last month. *(To* GREENE.*)* Right?

GREENE
(Stands up on the chair.) You're asking me? I'm only the club president. Yakubski is the treasurer. Ask him. He knows . . . maybe.

YAKUBSKI
What do you mean, "Maybe"?

GREENE
Nothing. Proceed.

SHALLECK
Hey, you! Get off the chair. Clean off the chair! *(Gives* GREENE *a rag to wipe the chair clean.)*

GREENE
Oops! Sorry. OK! I'll clean it.

YAKUBSKI
(To GREENE.*)* Sure, no problem. I'll submit the financial report to the Board.

GRADY
Can I make an announcement?

YAKUBSKI
(To GRADY.*)* Sure! Come up here.

GRADY
(Walks down the aisle. To FUTRELL.*)* Shut up! Be quiet! *(Steps onto the dais. To* YAKUBSKI.*)* Tonight we are celebrating a special event—Yakubski's birthday. This guy is 50 years old, but he still looks 35. How do you manage it? Congratulations!!! *(*ALL *clap their hands.)* And on behalf of our membership I want to thank you for your 30 years of faithful service to the club.

YAKUBSKI
How thoughtful of you all. *(Pause.)* I don't know how to thank you. . . .

KLAYMANS, SHALLECK, WISEMAN
Open it!

YAKUBSKI
(Unwraps the gift. Extracts a giant fountain pen.) Beautiful!!! Thanks, folks!!!

GRADY
So you can keep the accounts in figures large enough for all of us to read! And to show a profit!

(**EVERYONE** *applauds. Most of them stand up to cheer.* **GRADY** *especially cheers with great gusto!*)

YAKUBSKI
That's all. Now go have coffee or a drink or go to the restroom!

(*People carry their chairs to tables in the foreground, and some sit down while others cluster at the bar.* **MACHER, MCALLISTER,** *and* **YAKUBSKI** *stand in the foreground.*)

MACHER
(*To* **YAKUBSKI,** *clapping* **MCALLISTER** *on the shoulder.*) He's a fine player. He always sinks a basket. The defense can't stop him. I was the one who first recognized his potential when he was a boy in school. I've worked hard with him for years and years, and now it's beginning to pay off. (*To* **MCALLISTER.**) Right?

MCALLISTER
Yes, "Daddy." I really thank you. (**MACHER** *gives him a bearhug.*)

MACHER
Our team would be losers without you. If you could hear—bet you'd be on a pro team by now. For sure, semi-pros. Maybe the NBA. Who knows?

YAKUBSKI
(*To* **MACHER.**) Maybe we should try to help him. My cousin knows a pro player. They played together in high school. Maybe I could . . .

MACHER
(*Interrupting.*) That would be nice, but you know it's only a dream.

No hearing team will take a deaf player. "You can't hear the coach or the referee." That's what they always say. What a shame! You could help any team win the world championship!

McALLISTER
That's OK. I'll live. I get along fine.

MACHER
That's the spirit. C'mon, let's have something to drink.

McALLISTER
Sure. *(They approach the section of the bar where* **MRS. YAKUBSKI** *presides.)*

MACHER
(To **MRS. YAKUBSKI.***)* Hi, two 7-ups, please. *(***MACHER** *pays her.)*

MRS. YAKUBSKI
(To **McALLISTER.***)* Sure. No whiskey for you. You're a nice boy.

McALLISTER
That's me! Right!

MACHER
He's in training for the tournament. Reminds me of my own days of glory. Do you remember 30 years ago I helped the club team win the championship? Gary is following in my footsteps. *(***MRS. YAKUBSKI** *brings two 7-ups to* **MACHER** *and* **McALLISTER.** *To* **McALLISTER** *who drinks his 7-up.)* You've really got to go home soon. You need some sleep.

McALLISTER
Don't hurry me. Give me a little time to relax and enjoy myself.

GRADY
(To **LINDSEY** *who watches him work on the projector.)* Hi! Like the movie?

(**SPENCER COLLINS** *sits, watching them talk.*)

LINDSEY
Could be better. This projector must be over 20 years old.

GRADY
Almost 15.

LINDSEY
What a beat-up old machine. At Gallaudet I used to operate the
latest Bell & Howell, fully automatic. You just push in the film,
and it loads itself and runs so smoothly.

GRADY
We're not rich here. We bought this projector used, and it's still
running good enough. We don't need a machine that runs so
smooth. Anyway, I hear that then the film gets jammed and torn.
Say, you use some strange signs.

LINDSEY
What do you mean, strange?

(**MRS. GREENE** *brings a card table to set up on the dais.*)

GRADY
(*To* **LINDSEY**.) You fingerspell[9] big words. "Operate, opretate." I
don't know how to spell it. And you use fancy signs.

LINDSEY
That's Gallaudet sign language. It's national. Many of your signs
are colloquialisms or local dialect.

GRADY
You sure do use big words. What are those last three words? Our
signs are good enough for us. I'm older than you, so let me give
you some advice. You came here to make some new friends, right?

(LINDSEY nods.) If you want to be accepted, don't act like a smart-ass, or you won't make any friends. I don't mean to preach at you.

LINDSEY
Thanks for the advice. But what this place needs is more culture. *(LINDSEY turns around and looks at SPIVEY who grins and nods his head in return. LINDSEY spreads and drops his arms in a gesture of disgust. To GRADY.)* I'd like to make some changes to bring this place up to a higher level. *(Seeing that GRADY still does not understand.)* Oh, what's the use of talking to you? *(LINDSEY starts to walk away from GRADY while GRADY looks on puzzled and puts away the projector.)*

GRADY
(Stopping LINDSEY.) You're too hard-headed. No point in telling you what to do.

(COLLINS leaves the scene.)

YAKUBSKI
(Sits down by the table waving at LINDSEY.) Hi! Enjoying yourself? C'mon, have a drink.

LINDSEY
Yes, please.

(YAKUBSKI signals at SHALLECK to come over. SHALLECK does so.)

LINDSEY
(Fingerspells to SHALLECK.) Tom Collins!

(SHALLECK shakes his head, showing that he doesn't understand LINDSEY. YAKUBSKI talks in picture signs to SHALLECK who grins and shakes his head and points to two bottles on the shelf.)

SHALLECK
Don't have. First or second?

YAKUBSKI
(To SHALLECK.*)* The first one. *(To* LINDSEY.*)* We don't have any
fancy drinks here, just Scotch or Vodka. Scotch OK?

LINDSEY
OK, I'll take Scotch.

*(*YAKUBSKI *pays* SHALLECK, *and* SHALLECK *moves slowly toward
the bar, still watching them talk to each other.)*

LINDSEY
(To YAKUBSKI.*)* What's the matter with this bartender? Doesn't
he read fingerspelling?

YAKUBSKI
(To LINDSEY.*)* Shh! Be quiet!

SHALLECK
(Moves angrily toward LINDSEY *and taps him roughly on the
shoulder.)* You think I'm dumb? I have a house, a wife, children,
and a car. What've you got?

LINDSEY
OK, OK. Let's not make a big deal out of it.

COLLINS
(After SHALLECK *departs toward the bar, signs clumsily to* LINDSEY.*)*
I saw you spell my name, Collins. Just kidding, but my last name
is Collins, too.

LINDSEY
So?

COLLINS
Hi! What's your name? *(Flips a plastic cup into the air and catches
it.)*

LINDSEY
Mark Lindsey.

COLLINS
Hold it. Slow down, please.

LINDSEY
M-A-R-K. *(COLLINS bends his head trying to lipread LINDSEY. LINDSEY stands up and fingerspells.)* L-I-N-D-S-E-Y. *(Says, with exaggerated mouthing.)* Mark Lindsey *(Comes close to COLLINS.)* Where do you come from?

COLLINS
An oral school, but now I'm anxious to learn signs.

LINDSEY
(Whispers to YAKUBSKI.) Oh, a hippopotamus![10]

YAKUBSKI
(Whispers to LINDSEY.) Be nice to him. He's a good kid. No reason to be rough.

COLLINS
(Referring to "hippopotamus.") What did you say?

(LINDSEY ignores him. SHALLECK brings drinks. LINDSEY holds a paper cup with one hand and moves away.)

MRS. GREENE
(Interrupts and pats SHALLECK on the cheek. To SHALLECK.) Don't forget, skit practice Sunday afternoon.

SHALLECK
Yes, I know! *(SHALLECK walks toward the bar. WISEMAN clumsily grabs at SHALLECK's shirt. A stool falls.)*

WISEMAN
(To SHALLECK.*)* Another drink.

SHALLECK
No, I already gave you two.

KLAYMANS
(To WISEMAN.*)* He's right. You've had enough. Be careful.

WISEMAN
Only one more—and I promise it will be my last. After that, no more for me. Just one more.

KLAYMANS
NO! *(To* SHALLECK *who comes out from behind the bar.)* Don't give her any more. I'll take care of her.

SHALLECK
You better.

KLAYMANS
I'll be responsible for her. I'll take care of her. *(*KLAYMANS *moves forward, closer to* SHALLECK. *He pulls down the front of* KLAY-MAN'S *dress with a long-handled bar spoon to reveal her decolletage.)* Stop that! You've got nerve doing that. What'll your wife say?

SHALLECK
(Grinning.) She's not here tonight.

KLAYMANS
I'll tell her if you don't stop bothering me.

SHALLECK
Take it easy. I didn't mean anything.

KLAYMANS
(Angrily at **SHALLECK.***)* Keep your hands to yourself! *(Moves toward* **WISEMAN.***)* Come on. *(Leads* **WISEMAN** *back to the bar.)*

(The **FUTRELLS** *enter and greet* **YAKUBSKI.** **MRS. FUTRELL** *asks to see his pen. He takes it out of his shirt pocket to show her.)*

FUTRELL
(Stands and observes the doorbell flasher[11] carefully. To **YAKUBSKI.***)* Hi! Hey, look at those wires for the flasher. They're a fire hazard! This place would never pass a fire inspection.

YAKUBSKI
So—go ahead and fix it.

FUTRELL
Let me see . . . very strange. Who installed it?

YAKUBSKI
Grady.

FUTRELL
It shouldn't work at all. What a mess!

YAKUBSKI
Been working fine for four years now.

FUTRELL
You made a big mistake in ordering this equipment. It isn't UL approved. It isn't safe. It could short out and start a fire anytime.

MRS. FUTRELL
That Grady is really making money off the deaf. Just imagine, the other day he told a friend of mine that he was not in the doorbell business to make money but to help the deaf. What a hypocrite!

FUTRELL
Hush, dear, be careful!

YAKUBSKI
You heard wrong. Grady put in this system without charging the club.

MRS. FUTRELL
Really! Oops! I didn't know that. Sorry.

GRADY
(Interrupts **FUTRELLS** *and* **YAKUBSKI.***)* Hi! *(Senses something fishy in their reactions. To* **YAKUBSKI.***)* What's the matter?

FUTRELL
(Interrupts. To **GRADY.***)* This system shouldn't be working at all, but it does. I'm puzzled.

GRADY
Just my magic. Let me show you this wiring. It runs to the Sears transmitter under the bar. The receiver is hooked to the doorbell. *(Shows them how he did the wiring all the way to the bar. As the* **FUTRELLS** *and* **YAKUBSKI** *bend down to follow* **GRADY,** *his out-stretched hand happens to graze* **MRS. WISEMAN'S** *foot.)*

WISEMAN
(Jumps off the stool.) Eek! A mouse!

*(***KLAYMANS** *panics, too.)*

GRADY
(To **KLAYMANS.***)* I'm not a mouse. Just the flasher.

KLAYMANS
(Laughs. To **WISEMAN.***)* Oh, it's only the light flasher.

WISEMAN
Oh, it got me scared for nothing.

(KLAYMANS and WISEMAN return to their stools. GRADY, the FU-TRELLS, and YAKUBSKI move toward center of stage.)

FUTRELL
How many wireless receivers in this room?

GRADY
Four. By the way, I heard you lost your job. Is it true?

FUTRELL
Boy, news sure travels fast in the deaf world. Yes, I was laid off last week, after 15 years. So I started looking for a new job. I went to a place that advertised for skilled car mechanics. There were five other applicants, all hearing except me. They were snot-noses, fresh from school. I filled out the application form, but they hired one of those green kids. They said the job required a lot of talking, and a deaf man couldn't handle it. Bullshit! I told them no engine ever talked to anybody, and that I understood cars better than most hearing mechanics. *(To YAKUBSKI who stands by listening.)* They gave me the brushoff—nice, polite, regretful, but a brushoff all the same. They didn't want to be bothered.

YAKUBSKI
I know how you feel.

MRS. FUTRELL
(To YAKUBSKI.) Please help my husband. Can you do something?

YAKUBSKI
Well, I'm not a lawyer, but I understand there are new government laws, like Section 504,[12] that say deaf people have equal rights. I'll give you the business card of a man to see. If anyone can help, he can. *(YAKUBSKI hands the business card to FUTRELL. MRS. FUTRELL snatches it and looks at it.)*

MRS. FUTRELL
(Gives the card to FUTRELL. *Moves toward* YAKUBSKI.*)* You always help the deaf. Thank you for trying to help my husband.

YAKUBSKI
I do what I can. I only wish I could help him more.

FUTRELL
(To YAKUBSKI.*)* I feel like the frog in the joke. You know that joke?

YAKUBSKI
No, tell me.

MRS. FUTRELL
Oh, what a bore! I've already heard that joke a hundred times. Well, I'm going to sit down. *(Sits down and looks away.)*

FUTRELL
A scientist yelled "Jump!" at a frog, and it jumped. Then he cut off a leg and yelled again. It jumped once more. He repeated the experiment until all the four legs were cut off. The frog couldn't jump then, no matter how loud the scientist yelled. So he said, "The frog can't jump, because it's deaf." I'm just like the frog, because I'm deaf, too.

GRADY
I don't understand. *(While* YAKUBSKI *laughs hard.)*

FUTRELL
(To YAKUBSKI.*)* The hearies always try to keep the deaf down. I'm mad as hell.

YAKUBSKI
(To FUTRELL.*)* I don't blame you for feeling like that.

GRADY
(By then GRADY *understands. To* FUTRELL *and* YAKUBSKI *while* MRS. FUTRELL *looks on.)* I have story, too. I have a friend who is a printer. He inserts papers with both hands into a printing press. Well, one day as he was doing this, he happened to talk with another deafie, and, as he looked at that deafie, he mechanically put both hands into the machine and left them there just an instant too long. He yelled and screamed, and people rushed in and pulled him away. But it was too late, and his hands were crushed. They took him to a hospital. When his wife visited him in the hospital, his hands were bandaged. The doctors told him they weren't sure how his hands would heal. Well, finally after a week, they took the bandages off, and he found that only the middle fingers on both hands had been saved. So now he signs using only his middle fingers. His wife had to get used to his talking to her that way, with his middle fingers: "Good morning." "Let's have breakfast." "Is that coffee ready?" "You bring it to me." "I'm thirsty." *(Looks at his listeners who listen to* GRADY *seriously, except* MRS. FUTRELL *who laughs hysterically.)* You really believed that?

(They all look shocked, then burst into laughter.)

FUTRELL
You sure fooled me.

YAKUBSKI
You fooled me too. That was a great joke.

GRADY
If you hadn't told me about the frog, maybe I couldn't have fooled you. It just goes to show that the hearies always mess you up. Either you have no job at all, or you get a job and become crippled. *(*ALL *laugh.* FUTRELLS *move toward the bar, and* GRADY *says to* KLAYMANS *as she passes by.)* Hi, darling, where are you going?

KLAYMANS

What's that to you? I'm not going your way.

GRADY

You always give a clever answer. Well, I just like to talk with you, just to look at you.

KLAYMANS

And that's all you'll get, just a look. So long. *(She goes to the bathroom.)*

LINDSEY

(Walks backward, looking in **KLAYMAN'S** *direction as she passes him by, and bumps into* **GRADY.** *To* **GRADY.)** Oops! She's sure a looker. Who's she?

GRADY

That's Shirley Klaymans.

LINDSEY

Would you introduce me to her?

GRADY

OK, when she passes by on her way back.

LINDSEY

Fine, I appreciate it.

GRADY

She was recently divorced, for the third time. So you may have a chance. But she's a famous tease, and she doesn't go with just anyone, only with men she likes. So it'll be up to you.

LINDSEY

I accept the challenge. I'll wait until she comes back. *(Pause.)* Say, I just moved into my new apartment, and I need someone to put a doorbell flasher system in. Can you do it?

GRADY

Sorry, but I'm not in that business any more. Do you see that guy I just talked with? The tall one with long sideburns? That's Futrell, the TTY repairman. He can do it for you. *(To* FUTRELL *as* YAKUBSKI *departs.)* Hi, I'm bringing you new business. Mark Lindsey, here, from Gallaudet, needs your help to put flashing lights in his new apartment. (**GRADY** *leaves to join* **MRS. WISEMAN** *at the bar.)*

GREENE

(Enters from the right side of stage—the office. He picks up the jacket lying on the chair, investigates, brushes it, and starts to ask around.) Whose jacket is it?

FUTRELL

Pleased to meet you.

LINDSEY

Likewise. I need a good doorbell flasher system for my apartment.

FUTRELL

I recommend a wireless remote control flasher. Its advantage is that you can take it with you when you move to a new place.

LINDSEY

I don't want any wiring to be seen.

FUTRELL

Right, the only wiring needed is from the door frame to the doorbell button . . .

*(***LINDSEY** *notices* **GREENE***, interrupts and pushes* **FUTRELL** *aside and moves toward* **GREENE***.)*

GREENE

Is this jacket yours?

LINDSEY
Yes.

GREENE
Hang it up, over there. Our club has a rule: a fine of 75 cents for leaving jackets on chairs. I'll overlook it now, but don't do it again.

LINDSEY
I'll hang it up now. Where? *(Pause.)* Oh, there! *(On the way to hang up his jacket, collides with* **BALLIN.***)* Can't you see where you're going?

BALLIN
(Motions **LINDSEY** *to face him.)* Sorry. Hi, I'm Alan Ballin. Where are you from?

LINDSEY
Gallaudet College. I'm very pleased to meet you. *(Aside to* **FUTRELL** *who is sitting by the table.)* Tunnel vision?

*(***FUTRELL*** nods.)*

LINDSEY
(Aside to **YAKUBSKI.***)* I haven't the patience to talk with him.

BALLIN
College?! You must be very smart.

LINDSEY
(To **BALLIN.***)* What did you say?

BALLIN
(To **LINDSEY.***)* You must be very smart.

LINDSEY
(Uncomfortably.) Thank you. Nice to meet you. How wonderful that we can communicate! *(To* YAKUBSKI.*)* What a bore! *(To* BALLIN.*)* Excuse me now, see you later. *(Hangs up his jacket.)*

*(*KLAYMANS *passes by.* GRADY *stops her.* YAKUBSKI *leaves the scene, stage right.)*

GRADY
(To LINDSEY.*)* Let me introduce you. Mark Lindsey, meet Shirley Klaymans.

KLAYMANS
Pleased to meet you.

*(*GRADY *behind* KLAYMANS' *back signs* "Good luck" *to* LINDSEY.*)*

LINDSEY
(Moves with KLAYMANS *toward the center of the stage. Looks at* GRADY. KLAYMANS *looks around, missing* GRADY'S *message, then turns back to* LINDSEY.*)* Pleased to meet you, too. You look familiar. Didn't I see you last Friday at the tournament?

KLAYMANS
Yes—I was there, but I didn't see you.

LINDSEY
So now we've met. Better late than never, eh? Where are you from?

KLAYMANS
Louisiana. I'm a Southern belle. But I've been here for a long time now. I like it here. Excuse me now.

LINDSEY
See you later? Maybe we could have a drink together?

KLAYMANS
Yes, maybe later. Bye-bye now. *(She rejoins* WISEMAN, *is accosted by* BRANNON *who has been hovering on stage left.)*

BRANNON
Hi! That's a nice dress you have. Let me feel it. *(She fingers the material sensuously.* KLAYMANS *firmly removes* BRANNON'S *hands.)* You have good taste. (BRANNON *straddles a chair.)*

KLAYMANS
Thank you.

BRANNON
Could I buy you a drink?

KLAYMANS
No, thank you. I still haven't finished mine.

BRANNON
I often think about you. I came here tonight hoping to find you here.

KLAYMANS
Oh, really?

BRANNON
Yes, really. This place is so boring. Say, let's go out together somewhere. How about a show?

(WISEMAN *approaches* KLAYMANS *and her right hand rests on* KLAYMANS' *left shoulder.)*

KLAYMANS
No, thank you. Janice is here with me, and I can't leave her.

BRANNON
Well, perhaps some other time.

KLAYMANS
I'm always pretty busy but thanks anyway. Bye.

(BRANNON moves away.)

WISEMAN
Why didn't you tell her to go to hell and stop bothering you?

KLAYMANS
Oh, I feel sorry for her. . . . *(KLAYMANS pulls WISEMAN by her left arm back toward the bar.)*

WISEMAN
(Shoves KLAYMANS.) I'm not a Lesbian.

KLAYMANS
(Staring at MRS. FUTRELL who is talking to IDA YAKUBSKI.) Hold it! *(Trying to catch WISEMAN'S attention.)*

MRS. FUTRELL
(To IDA YAKUBSKI.) I always knew that Shirley Klaymans was a whore, but now she's mixing with Lesbians, too. How dare she? She's really shameless. She opens her legs to anyone. The slut! What's the world coming to?!

MRS. YAKUBSKI
(Spots KLAYMANS about to approach; to MRS. FUTRELL.) Shhh! Be quiet! Stop it!

KLAYMANS
(Taps MRS. FUTRELL'S shoulder.) I saw you call me a whore. That's too much!! You're always gossiping about me behind my back.

MRS. FUTRELL
I said nothing. I wasn't talking about you. I was talking about someone else. And you had no right to snoop in our conversation.

KLAYMANS

Liar! You old bitch! You're jealous of me because you're so fat, and ugly, and old!

MRS. FUTRELL

How awful! *(Runs toward* MR. FUTRELL.*)* Help! Protect me!

FUTRELL

What's wrong?

MRS. FUTRELL

She's attacking me! She called me awful names! Help! Don't just stand there!

(A crowd collects as MRS. FUTRELL *and* KLAYMANS *wrestle.* YAKUBSKI, SHALLECK, *and* GREENE *separate the two women.* GREENE *tries to get their attention.)*

YAKUBSKI

(To KLAYMANS.*)* Pipe down!

KLAYMANS

I'm fed up. *(To* MRS. FUTRELL.*)* Stop talking against me behind my back. You bitch! I warn you for the last time.

YAKUBSKI

There now, my dear. Don't excite yourself.

GREENE

(Standing between the two arguing women.) Quiet! No fighting in the club. Settle your differences outside!

*(*YAKUBSKI, *leaving* KLAYMANS, *comes across* LINDSEY. KLAYMANS, GREENE, *and the* FUTRELLS *leave.)*

LINDSEY

(To **YAKUBSKI.***)* What kind of cavemen do you have here? What animals! I miss Gallaudet with its cultured, high-class people.

YAKUBSKI

(To **LINDSEY.***)* If you keep talking like that, deaf people will ostracize you. For a deaf person, that's the end. A hearing person can go anywhere and establish a new life, but a deaf person's reputation will precede him. He'll be shunned by the deaf everywhere. That's the worst thing that can happen to a deaf man, so be careful what you say. (**LINDSEY** *goes off stage and* **YAKUBSKI** *follows him.)*

GRADY

(To **BRANNON.***)* Boy, that Futrell woman! She's impossible! Hi! Have you forgotten to say, "Hi"? Haven't seen you for a long time. Where have you been hiding yourself?

BRANNON

Hi! I've been busy. But tonight I decided I needed some company for a change.

GRADY

I won't ask what you were busy with. I don't shove my nose in other people's private affairs. Say, how are your dogs? Still walking them every night?

BRANNON

Yes, they must be missing me right now. And my cats probably miss me, too.

GRADY

I know what an animal lover you are.

(**BRANNON** *notices and tells* **GRADY** *that* **MRS. YAKUBSKI** *is waving at him across the floor.* **MRS. YAKUBSKI** *asks* **GRADY** *to play cards* *with her group.* YAKUBSKI *and* LINDSEY *enter and approach* BRANNON.*)*

YAKUBSKI
(To LINDSEY.*)* This girl is from Gallaudet. Let me introduce you. *(To* BRANNON.*)* Hi there. This is Mark Lindsey. *(To* LINDSEY.*)* Mary Brannon. You both are from Gallaudet. You have plenty to talk about. *(*YAKUBSKI *moves away.)*

LINDSEY
When did you graduate?

BRANNON
I didn't graduate. I dropped out.

LINDSEY
Oh, OK . . . Hope you're happy now.

BRANNON
What does it matter to you whether I'm happy or not?

FUTRELL
(Announcing to EVERYBODY.*)* Peace! Peace! Now we have peace. Look at them.

*(*KLAYMANS *and* MRS. FUTRELL *enter, chatting amiably.* GREENE *follows them.)*

GREENE
(Interrupts BRANNON.*)* This is the fourth time you've come here. A non-member may visit the club only three times a year. This is your fourth time, so you have to pay two dollars. *(*BRANNON *hands him two dollars wordlessly. He thanks her.)* You know now that you can't come here again unless you are a member.

BRANNON
Oh, right! OK, I'll think about it.

GREENE

Now you know. And don't be so sure it's so easy to become a member! *(Leaves* BRANNON *and walks toward bar.)*

*(*LINDSEY *at the bar beckons to* KLAYMANS *and both walk toward left of center stage.)*

LINDSEY

(To KLAYMANS.*)* You really gave it to that woman good. I support you.

KLAYMANS

Shhh! Let's not talk about it. She spreads gossip like poison.

*(*WISEMAN *follows* KLAYMANS *and nudges her, asking to be introduced.)*

KLAYMANS

(To LINDSEY.*)* This is my friend. *(To* WISEMAN.*)* Mark Lindsey, meet Janice Wiseman.

WISEMAN

Hi, pleased to meetcha. *(*WISEMAN *raises her right hand to be shaken. But* LINDSEY *ignores her, pulls* KLAYMANS *further apart from her, and continues talking to* KLAYMANS.*)*

LINDSEY

(To KLAYMANS.*)* I'm still sure we met before. At the NAD Convention in Cincinnati?

KLAYMANS

Ha, ha! No. I never went there. Many girls must look like me. I must look very ordinary.

LINDSEY

You're kidding. No one else looks like you. I'd recognize you anywhere.

KLAYMANS
You sure know how to talk smooth to women. This is your first visit to the club? Do you like it here?

LINDSEY
Well, I don't know. You see, the deafies here are low-class. I have a college degree. Of course, I don't mean you yourself are low-class. You look smart. Why didn't you go to college?

KLAYMANS
Well, . . . my English is not so good,[13] and besides I had to find a job. I never had the time to take the college entrance examinations.

LINDSEY
I can help you. I would be happy to prepare you for the exams.

KLAYMANS
That's nice of you, but I really don't have time to study for the entrance exam. Anyway, I am no longer a young girl.

LINDSEY
Don't kid me. You can't be more than 25.

KLAYMANS
Flatterer, I'm 31. You know the deaf always look younger than the hearing.

LINDSEY
I can't believe it. *(Observes her body.)* You look so young. What's the difference, a few years more or less? We're in the same generation. Let's have a drink. (**BOTH** *go toward the bar.)*

SHALLECK
(After serving **LINDSEY** *and* **KLAYMANS,** *walks over to* **YAKUBSKI.)**
That college snob is trying to make up to Klaymans. I'd like to wring his neck.

YAKUBSKI

What concern is that of yours? You're not married to Klaymans. You have a wife of your own.

SHALLECK

I just don't like it. Lindsey thinks this place is too low-class for him, and now he's trying to steal the best looking woman around here. Even if I am a married man, I can't help resenting it. *(Reverts to his customary good mood.)* She's so sexy-looking that I get excited when she comes near me. *(Mimes his excitement graphically.)*

YAKUBSKI

Ha, ha! You should be on TV. How are you getting along with your boss now? *(SHALLECK and YAKUBSKI move toward left of stage.)*

SHALLECK

Don't talk to me about him. He thinks I'm worthless. He treats me like dirt beneath his feet. He makes me eat shit. He orders me around. And every week he takes out most of the money I've earned from my paycheck—for taxes, Social Security, health insurance—stuff like that. I'm getting fed up. *(CARSWELL stands, watching them talk; as SHALLECK swings his right arm to sign "fed up," he accidentally slams CARSWELL in the chest.)* Oh! Sorry!

CARSWELL

That's OK. Just watch out next time.

(As CARSWELL and YAKUBSKI sit down at a table, SPENCER COLLINS leaves the bar, walks up to CARSWELL, and taps him on the shoulder.)

COLLINS

(To CARSWELL.) Someone told me that you sell ABC cards. Is that true?

*(*YAKUBSKI *gestures* "Quiet" *behind* CARSWELL'S *back to* COLLINS.*)*

CARSWELL
So what! Is that any of your business?

COLLINS
Our business! *(Pause.)* Yes! *(Pause.)* All of us here are deaf, too. You got nerve to come here when you are spoiling the name of us deaf by begging.

CARSWELL
Damn hippopotamus! I don't like the way you talk.

COLLINS
I'm not a hippopotamus any more. I'm deaf, too, and I'm a better deaf person than you.

CARSWELL
Maybe so, but I'm richer. Do you see this fist? Want a black eye? I'll teach you to respect me. *(*CARSWELL *grabs the front of* COLLINS' *shirt, and they scuffle a little before* GREENE, YAKUBSKI, *and* SHAL-LECK *separate them.* YAKUBSKI *leads* COLLINS *to a seat at the table.* SHALLECK *takes* CARSWELL *over to the opposite side of the stage, away from the table.)*

YAKUBSKI
(To COLLINS.*)* What's got into you? I'm surprised at you.

COLLINS
How dare that beggar, that repulsive creature come here and mix with us!

YAKUBSKI
(Mouths words at COLLINS.*)* What gives you the right to speak for all deaf people? You think he isn't one of us? How do you know? What makes you so sure?

COLLINS
But how can you all accept a man who spoils the name of the deaf? He makes hearing people despise deaf people.

GREENE
(Puts cigar on edge of table, mouths words at COLLINS.*)* We accept him. You can see for yourself; he is here. We didn't kick him out! But we could kick you out for causing a disturbance!

YAKUBSKI
The hearies already think so little of the deafies, what's the difference? What's more, we think a lot of Carswell. He's a big man here. He makes more money than all the other people here. We respect him because he fools the hearies. They always take advantage of the deaf, but that peddler, a deafie, takes advantage of them for a change. Can't you see that?

COLLINS
I don't want to argue. Forget it.

GREENE
Go apologize to Carswell.

COLLINS
That's too much! I can't do it.

GREENE
Out you go!

YAKUBSKI
(Shushing GREENE.*)* Look, Collins is just naive and doesn't know any better. *(To* COLLINS.*)* You want to be one of us? Then do as we do. We accept you—you accept Carswell. You insulted him. Now go and say you're sorry.

GRADY
(Butting in. To COLLINS.*)* Please say "sorry" to Carswell. *(Mouths words badly.)*

COLLINS
Oh, well, OK. *(Gets up and approaches* CARSWELL. *Taps him lightly on shoulder.* CARSWELL *reacts nervously and quickly, on the defensive.)* Forget it?

CARSWELL
(Expresses himself orally to COLLINS.*)* That's OK, man. I understand. I know you come from the oral world and still don't understand the deaf, but that will come in time. Don't worry. *(Slaps table loudly with both hands.)* Drinks on the house!

*(*EVERYONE *claps and rushes to the bar, leaving* CARSWELL *and* COLLINS *alone.)*

COLLINS
I thought you were . . .

CARSWELL
You're not the only one to think of me like that. It's the deaf teachers and other high-class snobs who hate me the most. But they can go amuse themselves. Average deaf people accept me and understand. And that's good enough for me. I know you still don't understand all I say. Well, don't worry about that. You'll learn.

*(*SHALLECK *and* GREENE *bring drinks to* CARSWELL *and* COLLINS. ALL *gather around them.)*

GRADY
(Hollers.) To Deaf Power!! *(Makes an upraised "protest" fist with one hand while the other hand covers his ear.)*

(ALL raise the paper cups into the air and give the Deaf Power salute. YAKUBSKI, GREENE, COLLINS, SHALLECK, and CARSWELL touch cups as if they were clinking glasses. The lights go down.)

End of Act One

Bartender Tim Shalleck
(Charles Buemi) serves club
members *left to right* Shirley
Klaymans (Eileen Bechara),
Janice Wiseman (Nancy
Torbett), and Abe Greene
(Thomas Janulewicz).

Spencer Collins (Thomas
Fields), finding it difficult to
follow a conversation, exclaims,
"Hold it. Slow down, please."

Jean Futrell (Adele Shuart) watches sceptically as her husband tells a joke she has heard hundreds of times before.

Jim Yakubski (Robert Dillman) *center* exclaims to Collins Spencer (Thomas Fields) *seated,* "What's got into you?" while Abe Greene (Thomas Janulewicz) *right* and Mark Lindsey (William Ennis) *standing left* look on.

Jim Yakubski (Robert Dillman)
tells club members there are
important announcements at
the beginning of the meeting.

Shirley Klaymans (Eileen
Bechara) and Charles Carswell
(Richard K. Moore) listen atten-
tively to club announcements.

Mary Brannon (Georgetta Doran) nurses her drink alone and considers recent events at the club.

Mark Lindsey (William Ennis) *left* says to Alan Ballin (Stephen Kimble) *right*, "How wonderful we can communicate!"

Will Grady (Larry Berke) en-
tertains club members with his
story about the careless printer.

Winona Shoemaker (Elizabeth
Hathaway) meets Charles
Carswell (Richard K. Moore),
who offers the recent high
school graduate a job as his
assistant.

Jim Yakubski (Robert Dillman) *left* says regretfully, "No hearing team will take a deaf player," while Jay Macher (Frank Del Rosso) *center* and Gary McAllister (Steve Brunelle) *right* discuss his career in sports.

Thomas Spivey (Jerry Little) sits in isolation near the club jukebox.

ACT TWO

Setting as in Act One. Time: same evening, somewhat later. YAK-
UBSKI *and* CARSWELL *sit by the table on stage right.* BRANNON
sits drinking alone at a table on stage left.

YAKUBSKI
(To CARSWELL.*)* I need your advice. The club has money problems.
The landlord is raising our rent by $100 a month. We just raised
our club dues two months ago, and we can't do it again this year.
The members don't earn much. Coming here is their only pleasure.
But if we don't get that money, we'll be evicted.

CARSWELL
But didn't Futrell just say tonight that you've got enough in the
treasury?

YAKUBSKI
Futrell isn't the treasurer. I am. I know. There's not enough money.
Period.

CARSWELL
You want my advice? Go to that Deafness Research Institute for
help.

YAKUBSKI
(Gets up and walks toward the center of stage.) Never again! What
creeps they are. They set up a meeting of deaf leaders and asked
us how they could help the deaf. I said deaf people need more jobs,
and our club needs a better location and new furniture. But they
said they didn't mean that. Instead, they wanted to counsel us
about our emotional and social problems. You know Greene, our
club president? He likes plain talk. He got up and waved his cigar
and then chomped on it; he said we didn't need that kind of help,

and we didn't need anyone snooping around and following us, as if we were animals like Washoe, the chimpanzee.[14]

CARSWELL
Ha! ha! Beautiful! Greene sure told them off.

YAKUBSKI
Afterwards, outside, Greene was still boiling mad and told me he felt like telling those jerks they were the ones who needed emotional and social counseling, not us.

(**YAKUBSKI** *stealthily looks around.* **BRANNON'S** *and* **YAKUBSKI'S** *eyes meet.* **BRANNON** *then leaves her table and walks toward the bar.* **YAKUBSKI** *motions* **CARSWELL** *to move toward the left of center stage.*)

YAKUBSKI
To be honest, what I need from you isn't advice. Advice is cheap. I need $500. Can I borrow it from you? (*Pauses as* CARSWELL *is startled by this remark.*)

CARSWELL
(*Moves slowly toward the center of the stage, and turns to face* YAKUBSKI.) Why do you need that money?

YAKUBSKI
That's my business. Just say yes or no. (*Pauses.*) I'll pay you back in two weeks.

CARSWELL
The answer is no. You talk about the club's money problems, but you ask for a personal loan. There's some funny business going on. I know you're in trouble.

YAKUBSKI
What do you mean?

CARSWELL

You can't stop shit from stinking.

YAKUBSKI

Wait a minute. I'm interested. You can't get away from me after saying that. What do you mean?

CARSWELL

I saw you at the racetrack, betting at a $50 window. Where did you get that kind of money? How come you're suddenly a big spender?

YAKUBSKI

Are you a cop, asking me those questions?

CARSWELL

OK, I'll shut up. Everyone has his own problems. *(CARSWELL moves toward stage right while YAKUBSKI follows him.)*

YAKUBSKI

But, did you know that . . . ? *(He is distracted by seeing SHALLECK and a drunken WISEMAN moving toward the center; he approaches them.)*

SHALLECK

Help! I'm having trouble with Wiseman. She's getting drunk.

CARSWELL

(Taps YAKUBSKI's shoulder.) See what I mean? Everyone has his own problems.

(YAKUBSKI shrugs at him and tries to calm WISEMAN. SHALLECK departs.)

YAKUBSKI

(To MRS. WISEMAN.) My dear, you've had too much already. You can't have any more. It's against club rules.

MRS. WISEMAN

But my hands are shaking. I'm so upset. I just heard that woman, Futrell, has been spreading lies about me. She said I have roaches in my house. Now that my husband is dead, I don't have anyone to protect me from gossip. What about her? Her house is so dirty, decent people won't visit her. There's always a mess on the floor, and the windows are never clean; they're so dirty you can't see through them.

YAKUBSKI

Are you sure Mrs. Futrell said that thing about roaches?

MRS. WISEMAN

A friend told me so, and I believe her. Damn right!

YAKUBSKI

Maybe you heard wrong. Don't be so sure. Maybe things got twisted in the telling. You didn't *see* her say that?

MRS. WISEMAN

(Sits down.) No, but I believe she said it. Who does that bitch think she is? She always talks bad about other people. What's her problem?

YAKUBSKI

I'm sure she didn't mean it about you.

MRS. WISEMAN

She meant it! I'll never invite that woman to my house again.

YAKUBSKI

I have visited your house several times, and it has always been shining clean. I never saw any bugs.

MRS. WISEMAN

So you see what a liar that woman is!

MRS. GREENE
(To **MRS. WISEMAN**.*)* I'm worried about you. If you keep drinking, I can't let you act in the skits.

MRS. WISEMAN
No, no. Please don't!! I promise I won't touch a drop more.

MRS. GREENE
OK, but I'll be watching you. Take care.

MRS. WISEMAN
I promise, I promise.

MRS. YAKUBSKI
Here, dear, have some coffee to help you sober up.

*(***MRS. GREENE** *and* **MRS. YAKUBSKI** *lead* **MRS. WISEMAN** *toward the coffee urn.)*

GREENE
I saw you tell Yakubski that you saw him at the racetrack.

CARSWELL
What if I did see him there. It's not my business, anyhow.

GREENE
Maybe not, but it's our business. A treasurer isn't supposed to be a gambler. I know something I can't tell you; but believe me, it's vital that I know what happened at the track.

CARSWELL
Well, I can't tell you whether he won or lost. *(Stands up.)* Did you see our whole conversation?

GREENE
(Moves toward stage right.) No, Yakubski leaned over, so that I couldn't see what you said next.

CARSWELL

I got some more news for you, but only if you tell me why it's so important for you to know. Let's swap secrets.

GREENE:

It's a deal! OK, I'll tell you first. I've got reason to believe that Yakubski stole club money.

CARSWELL

Oh, wow! But I'm not really surprised. Now it all figures. OK, I'll tell you. Yakubski asked me for a personal loan of $500. Of course, I refused. I thought there was something fishy about it all.

GREENE

You're damn right something's fishy. Now I'm getting the whole picture.

(**YAKUBSKI** *enters from the right.* **CARSWELL** *warns* **GREENE** *of* **YAKUBSKI'S** *presence.*)

GREENE

(*To* **CARSWELL**.) Thanks for telling me, see you later.

(**CARSWELL** *sits down at stage right.*)

GREENE

(*Approaches* **YAKUBSKI** *near the table on stage left.*) I've got to talk with you. Let's sit down. This morning I got another bill that you were supposed to pay two months ago. (*Removes bill from pocket.*) Why didn't you send the goddam money? $150 for food and liquor for that dinner party the club gave in honor of my wife's 50th birthday. And the money is two months overdue. Two months!

YAKUBSKI

There must be some mistake. Give it to me. (*Examines the bill.*)

I can explain everything. Simple: I never got their first bill. It must have been sent to the wrong address.

GREENE

You mean you waited two months—two goddam months—to pay a bill? *(Stands up and bends forward.)* You should have paid on the spot! That's your job as a treasurer! Damn it, man! You know what we owe, and you're supposed to pay it. *(Sits down.)*

YAKUBSKI

What's wrong with waiting for the bill? Do you pay your debts before you get the bill? Hell, no! That's no way to do business.

GREENE

But it's bothering me. Why can't you pay the bill and get it over with?

YAKUBSKI

(Stands up and GREENE *stands up, too.)* Let me decide what's best. You're the president, and I don't tell you how to run meetings. I'm the treasurer, not you, and you can't tell me how to manage financial matters. I know what I'm doing.

GREENE

(Moves toward the right of center stage.) I understand there's something about horses in your life.

YAKUBSKI

(Looks surprised.) What do you mean? *(Approaches* GREENE.*)*

GREENE

Take it easy. I don't mean anything. Wait until the Board meeting. I'm only trying to do the best thing for the club.

YAKUBSKI

So am I.

GREENE

OK, no hard feelings. *(*GREENE *readily approaches* YAKUBSKI *to shake hands, and* YAKUBSKI *reacts reluctantly at first, but finally shakes his hand.* YAKUBSKI *leaves to approach* CARSWELL *while* GREENE *goes stage left.)*

YAKUBSKI

(Looks nervously in the direction of GREENE *three times while he's talking with* CARSWELL.*)* I saw you talk about horse races and mention my name to Greene. I spoke to you in confidence, but you repeated what I said to someone else. You're spreading rumors about me. I don't like it.

CARSWELL

Who? What? What are you talking about?

YAKUBSKI

You know very well what I'm talking about.

CARSWELL

No, I don't. I never name people. You must be imagining things. I think you need glasses—you can't see well.

YAKUBSKI

OK, OK, let's drop it. I'm disgusted. I don't feel like discussing it.

(Door light flashes. EVELYN JACKSON *and* WINONA SHOEMAKER *rush in, attracting the attention of almost* EVERYONE.*)*

JACKSON

(To YAKUBSKI.*)* Some hoodlums outside were bothering this girl. I wanted to help, but I was afraid—then I saw she was deaf—so I waded in and beat them with my handbag until they ran away.

YAKUBSKI
You're lucky nothing worse happened. *(To* **SHOEMAKER.***)* You're deaf?

SHOEMAKER
Yes, I'm deaf. I graduated from MSD last summer.

YAKUBSKI
(To the **CROWD.***)* Something should be done about those hoods outside. I'm going to complain to the police. *(To* **SHOEMAKER.***)* Welcome! I'm Jim Yakubski. Here you're among friends. Make yourself at home. *(To* **JACKSON.***)* Hi, Jackson, how have you been?

JACKSON
Just fine. It's so nice and warm here after the cold outside, br-r-r. I'd give a million dollars for a cup of hot coffee. *(To* **SHOE-MAKER.***)* Come, dear, take off your coat and have coffee with me. *(To* **IDA YAKUBSKI.***)* Can you get us some coffee, please?

IDA YAKUBSKI
(To **SHOEMAKER.***)* OK, where's the million? Cream and sugar?

SHOEMAKER
Do you have Coke?

IDA YAKUBSKI
Sure, we have Coke. Want one?

SHOEMAKER
Yes.

IDA YAKUBSKI
(To **JACKSON.***)* Sugar and cream?

JACKSON
Oh, just black, please. *(***JACKSON** *gives some money to* **IDA YAK-UBSKI.***)*

(IDA *departs.* JACKSON *leads* SHOEMAKER *stage right where the table and chairs are.* JACKSON *and* SHOEMAKER *sit down. Almost* EVERYONE *scatters to return to his or her place.)*

JACKSON
(To SHOEMAKER.*)* Not scared anymore? That was a bad experience for you. Never come to the club alone!

SHOEMAKER
Whew! For a moment I thought that hoodlum was going to mug me. Lucky thing you saw me and saved me. Thank you.

(MRS. YAKUBSKI *interrupts and brings the cup of coffee for* JACKSON *and a can of Coca Cola for* SHOEMAKER. MRS. GREENE *and* MRS. FUTRELL *are watching them talk.)*

JACKSON
Glad to help, dear. This area is becoming more and more dangerous. You shouldn't come here alone, you know. After the club closes, I'll walk you to your car.

SHOEMAKER
I have no car. I lost my license.

JACKSON
What happened?

SHOEMAKER
(Stands up and moves around as she talks to JACKSON.*)* Oh—I had the most horrible experience last week. I was driving around a traffic circle when another car smashed into mine and crumpled my fender. A woman was driving the other car. I was really mad. But she couldn't have been nicer—apologizing all over the place. Then a patrol car came by, and the cop told us to get in and tell him what happened. I told my story first, and then the other woman. She covered her mouth with her hand so I couldn't lipread

her. Made me so mad. I'm a good lipreader, but I couldn't get a
thing out of her. When she finally shut up, the cop wrote a ticket—
and gave it to me! Wasn't my fault at all! I still get furious when
I think of it! That was a cheap, dirty trick. She took advantage
of my deafness.

MACHER
(Breaking in.) Excuse me. *(To* **JACKSON.***)* Could you please make
a phone call for me?

JACKSON
(To **MACHER.***)* Sure! *(To* **SHOEMAKER.***)* Be back in a moment. My
poor dear, I sympathize with you. *(Leaves.)*

SHOEMAKER
What! Phone?! *(To* **MRS. GREENE.***)* Is that woman hearing?

MRS. GREENE
Yes, dear. Miss Jackson is hearing. Her parents were deaf, and
she loves to come to our club. She is a very nice woman and helps
us a lot by interpreting for us.

SHOEMAKER
Oh yes! It's wonderful of her to help the deafies.

MRS. GREENE
(To **SHOEMAKER.***)* Let me introduce you to the others.

*(***MRS. GREENE** *and* **SHOEMAKER,** *picking up her can of Coca Cola,
leave the scene.)*

CARSWELL
(Walks toward **BRANNON,** *who is sitting by the right side of table
at stage left.)* Hey, I saw you somewhere before.

BRANNON
You think so?

CARSWELL

Oh yes! Now I remember you. Three weeks ago I went into a restaurant and passed out my ABC cards to the people at the tables. When I came back to collect the money, you gave me a quarter. But you're deaf, yourself. Why give me money?

BRANNON

Because I wanted to.

CARSWELL

What crazy idea made you act like that in the restaurant, when you're deaf yourself?

BRANNON

OK, I'm crazy. Sometimes I really think I am.

GRADY

(Interrupts CARSWELL.*)* Keep cool. That's enough.

CARSWELL

(Pushes GRADY *aside. To* BRANNON.*)* You think I'm stupid? You think you're better than any of us because you're so smart? You insulted me. I have my pride, too. Here take your quarter back. *(Puts quarter on her right hand;* BRANNON *throws it to the floor.* CARSWELL *picks it up and throws it at her.)* I don't accept money from deaf people. *(*BALLIN *stumbles against him and falls.* CARSWELL *picks him up.)* Be careful!

BALLIN

(Brings his face closer to CARSWELL.*)* Oh, excuse me.

CARSWELL

(To BALLIN.*)* Watch where you're going. Why do you go out if you can't see where you're going?

BALLIN
(To CARSWELL.*)* If I stay home, I sit there all alone, talking to
myself. It bores me to death. I want to come here and be with
deaf people, no matter how difficult it is for me to communicate.
I can't see well. I can't help that. But it's enough for me just to
be with deaf people. You understand? *(*CARSWELL *stands silently
like a statue.)* Thank you. *(*BALLIN *leaves.)*

CARSWELL
(To GRADY.*)* How does that guy ever manage to find his way here
to the club?

GRADY
Yakubski drives him here. Poor Ballin. With his tunnel vision,
he's so lonely. We all like him. And that's Yakubski for you—
always helping somebody.

CARSWELL
To each his own. I could tell you plenty about Yakubski, but hell,
it's not my business.

GRADY
What do you mean? Tell me.

CARSWELL
Let's forget it. *(*GRADY *follows* CARSWELL *towards the bar to con-
tinue their discussion.)*

FUTRELL
(Calls excitedly to LINDSEY, GRADY, *and* CARSWELL, *as he enters
from stage left, waving a newspaper.)* Did you know the Supreme
Court is deaf?

LINDSEY
No. What do you mean? How do you know?

FUTRELL
(Displays a newspaper headline saying, "Supreme Court Deaf to Plea.") Here it says, "Supreme Court Deaf to Plea."

*(***BRANNON*** holds newspaper while* ***FUTRELL*** *speaks to* ***LINDSEY***.)

GRADY
(To ***LINDSEY***.) Futrell is right!

LINDSEY
(Half-embarrassed by ***FUTRELL'S*** *and* ***GRADY'S*** *ignorance as he moves around slowly.)* Don't you know how to read a newspaper? This means that the Supreme Court ignores or won't pay attention to a request. It is as if the court didn't hear it, or is "deaf" to it. Get it?

FUTRELL
(Mystified, shakes his head.) No.

LINDSEY
(To ***FUTRELL***.*)* No? You don't get it? Why do I waste my breath trying to explain things to you?

FUTRELL
(To ***LINDSEY*** *in an aggrieved tone.)* Because you've been to college, you always like to win arguments. It's no use talking to you. *(***FUTRELL*** leaves and the others follow him as the crowd breaks away, leaving* ***LINDSEY*** *alone as* ***BRANNON*** *approaches him.)*

BRANNON
(Laughs.) You better be careful what you say. Don't talk like a smart aleck to the others!

LINDSEY
(To ***BRANNON***.*)* Hey, what do you mean by "smart aleck"? *(***LINDSEY*** and* ***BRANNON*** move toward the bar.)*

KLAYMANS

(Stops **YAKUBSKI** *as he passes.)* Hi! Finally, we meet. Stop and talk with me a minute. Come on!

YAKUBSKI

I'm always running around like crazy. That Greene, he chomps on his fat cigar and talks big, but I'm the one who handles the club business, and I give people help when they need it.

KLAYMANS

(Pulls him by the wrist, walks toward the table located at stage left.) So stay with me a little and relax. *(***THEY*** sit.)*

YAKUBSKI

(Pause.) I hear you just got your divorce. Should I be happy or sad for you?

KLAYMANS

Happy! Jim, why is it I always marry the wrong man? Sam seemed so loving. *(Pause.)* He promised me everything. But right after the wedding he showed his real self—he turned out to be a real bastard. You know what the SOB did the first night we got back from our honeymoon? He really shocked me. He said a woman's place is at home, and he refused to help me cook or clean house. The bastard just lay on the sofa and watched TV and wouldn't even lift a hand while I slaved in the house. Aw—I should've known better, marrying a hearie. And he said he didn't want me coming here to the club because only low-class stupid deaf people sign. He calls deaf signers stupid. Hah! So I told Mr. High-and-Mighty that maybe I was stupid to be fooled by him so long. That shook him up! And I told the SOB to get out of my house! He blew up and called me everything you could think of—whore, slut . . . everything! *(Woebegone.)* Oh, Jim, all I want is a guy who'll be nice to me and not exploit me. Is that asking too much? Why do I always pick the wrong man?

YAKUBSKI
You had bad luck. It can't last forever.

KLAYMANS
Oh, Christ, I hope not! I haven't given up looking for the right man.

YAKUBSKI
I know. Maybe good luck is waiting for you.

KLAYMANS
He has to be a real man, though. That's what I need.

YAKUBSKI
Maybe that's your trouble.

KLAYMANS
(Slowly.) What do you mean?

YAKUBSKI
Shirley! Shirley! You're always looking for what you call a "real man." Well, "real" men always have to prove they're real men by chasing other women and by pushing you around. Maybe you'd be better off with a nice guy. A nice guy doesn't have to prove anything, so he has time to be nice to you.

KLAYMANS
A nice guy like you?

YAKUBSKI
Thank you for saying that! I needed that. I feel so low.

KLAYMANS
Oh, Jim. What is it? Can I help? *(YAKUBSKI gets up and KLAYMANS follows him.)*

YAKUBSKI

Never mind. I don't want to bother you with my problem. Talking about "real" men, what about that college boy over there? *(Points at* LINDSEY *while* YAKUBSKI *and* KLAYMANS *stand at the center stage.)* He's interested in you, I noticed. Maybe that's your man.

KLAYMANS

Lindsey? He's in love with himself! But maybe I'll have some fun with him, trying to puncture that swelled head of his while I'm waiting for Mr. Right to come along. But stop changing the subject. What's the matter? You look so desperate!

YAKUBSKI

Sorry I told you, but when you called me a nice guy . . .

KLAYMANS

(Interrupting.) But you are a nice guy! You know, . . .

YAKUBSKI

(Interrupting.) Nice guy—shit! I'm no good.

KLAYMANS

Stop talking like that. You're the best man I know—always helping, always . . .

YAKUBSKI

(Breaking in.) Shirley, I'm in trouble, deep trouble!

KLAYMANS

I know. I bet it's that no-good son of yours, the dope addict.

YAKUBSKI

Yes. This morning he showed up and demanded $50 for another fix. Ida got heart palpitations when she saw him. I don't want to talk about it anymore.

KLAYMANS

Oh, Jim. People always are running to you for help when they're in trouble, but when you need help you've got nobody to go to.

YAKUBSKI

Thanks for your sympathy, Shirley. But I'm stuck, and I can't see my way out. Shit, I've got other problems, too. That prick Greene is after me. He's my worst enemy and my chief rival as club leader. He's got something on me that I can't tell you about, and now he's going to cut my throat. I feel like I'm being buried alive.

KLAYMANS

It hurts me when you talk like that. Is it really that bad? I've got troubles, too, but yours seem worse. What can Greene have on you? You're a fine man and a good treasurer. And what does your son have to do with Greene? Nobody can blame you because your son can't kick the habit. I just don't understand. Is there anything I can do?

MRS. YAKUBSKI

(Interrupting. To **KLAYMANS**.*)* Hi, I see you want to steal my husband.

KLAYMANS

I'd like to, but he's too faithful to you.

MRS. YAKUBSKI

Ha, ha! Kathy Greene wants me to remind you to come and practice your skit Sunday at two, OK? I've got to rush and help Kathy cut the cake now. *(To* **YAKUBSKI**.*)* What's the matter with you?

YAKUBSKI

Nothing, darling. It's just that I'm totally exhausted. Let's go home soon.

MRS. YAKUBSKI

OK, dear, in a few minutes. You need your rest. I'll make some more coffee. Will you please help me lift the coffee urn? When we're finished, we can go.

YAKUBSKI

Sure! *(The* YAKUBSKIS *walk toward the coffee urn.)*

BRANNON

(Walks from the bar to stage left. LINDSEY *follows* BRANNON, *and they sit down. To* LINDSEY.*)* Cut it out! You ask too many questions.

LINDSEY

(To BRANNON.*)* Can I ask you just one more question?

BRANNON

Well?

LINDSEY

Why did you give the quarter to that ABC peddler?

BRANNON

That's none of your business, but OK, I'll try to answer. I was there with a hearing friend who was watching me to see what I would do. So I decided to be contrary and do what he would never expect me to do—give money to a deaf beggar. I also wanted to demonstrate how different I, as a deaf person, was from that beggar. I don't know, really. Now I've got mixed feelings about it.

LINDSEY

May I ask you another personal question?

BRANNON

You ask too many personal questions, but OK. That will be the last one.

LINDSEY

Fine. Why did you drop out of Gallaudet, or is it a secret?

BRANNON

Oh, no. I just got fed up. Just got the habit of not showing up on exam days. Know what my grade record was? I was on the dean's list one year—all straight A's—and all F's the next year. Nope, I didn't freak out. *(She laughs harshly.)* I just had no patience. Everything the teachers said was so predictable. And the campus atmosphere was just too sophomoric for me. So here I am. I'm a computer programmer now and make twice as much as anybody else, except that low-life ABC card peddler.

LINDSEY

I see you don't want to become a member of this club. Neither do I. But I am curious to know why you keep coming here.

BRANNON

(Ponders for awhile.) It's a love and hate relationship. The larger world—the hearing world—shuts me out, but I loathe the gossip and banalities that prevail in the small, constricted world of the deaf. At the same time, I'm attracted to the deaf. Why? Because they represent my last human contact. In spite of, or rather because of, their bluntness and candor they somehow seem more human than the hearing.

LINDSEY

Ha, ha! Meaning that you'll come here again for the fifth time, and the club president will make his little speech to you again, and you'll fork over another two bucks.

BRANNON

Well, I suppose you're right. Except that each time it will become a little worse. The deaf already view me as a deadbeat and a loner, which in fact I am. Do you see that man? *(Indicates* SPIVEY. SPIVEY *sees her point at him, gets up, and walks toward* BRANNON

and LINDSEY. BRANNON *motions him back toward his chair.* BRAN-
NON *throws a sardonic look at* LINDSEY.*)*

BRANNON
(To LINDSEY.*)* That's him. The one with the fixed grimace—like
a rictus—on his face. He never talks to anyone. They've given up
trying to talk to him. He just nods and grins in a way that gives
people the creeps, so now they avoid him. That's the club pariah.
I'll become more and more like him if I keep coming here. Yet I
can't help coming here. They're my last human contact. And I'm
becoming more inhuman, more and more detached from the others.

LINDSEY
Yes, I see. The deafies here are illiterate. That's why I'm not
going to join this club.

BRANNON
(Gets up.) Ah, it's no use talking to you. *(*BRANNON *walks away
and* LINDSEY *looks mystified.)*

*(*CARSWELL *leaves the bar and approaches* SHOEMAKER *who is
sitting with* MRS. FUTRELL, MRS. GREENE, *and* BALLIN. *He offers
a can of Coca Cola to* SHOEMAKER.*)*

CARSWELL
(Leads SHOEMAKER *away from the* CROWD *over to the left of center
stage; he places their drinks on the table.)* Hi, I'm Charlie Carswell.
What's your name?

SHOEMAKER
I'm Winona Shoemaker. Pleased to meet you. So this is the Club!
Now I'm finally here. When I was a little girl, I wanted to come
here, but they wouldn't let me except for Halloween parties. Now
I'm an adult and can come. How many members does this club
have?

CARSWELL

Oh, about a hundred. You are from the school for the deaf, right?
My little nephew goes there. Jimmy Carswell. Know him?

SHOEMAKER

Oh, yes, the one who always plays tricks on his teachers.

CARSWELL

Ha, ha! That's him; he's like me. Say, what are your plans now
that you've left school? Have you gotten a job?

SHOEMAKER

Yes, I'm a keypunch operator.

CARSWELL

You look like you can do much better. Now take me. I have my
own business, and I make plenty of money—as you can see from
my clothes.

SHOEMAKER

Yes, I like what you're wearing. You look real cool.

CARSWELL

(Smiles and looks nervously in EVELYN JACKSON'S *direction.)* I
could use a smart girl like you as my assistant.

SHOEMAKER

Oh? What would you expect me to do?

CARSWELL

I'd expect you to represent me. Come and see me about a job next
week, and then I'll tell you more. *(Hands her a business card.)*
How much are you making now?

SHOEMAKER

$140 a week. I'm an apprentice.

CARSWELL

(Glances nervously in EVELYN JACKSON'S *direction again. To* SHOEMAKER.*)* I'll pay you $300.

SHOEMAKER
(Surprised.) Oh! How sweet of you!

CARSWELL

No need to thank me. It's nothing. *(Seeing that* EVELYN JACKSON *is about to finish her telephone conversation.)* So I'll expect you in my office. When?

SHOEMAKER
I work until five but I'm free after that.

CARSWELL
Say, why not have dinner together?

SHOEMAKER
Sure, I'll be pleased to.

CARSWELL
How about Monday? Meet you at six at Harvey's? You know where it is, at LaSalle & 7th Street?

SHOEMAKER
But that's a fancy restaurant! OK, I'll meet you there.

CARSWELL
I got to go back to my friends now, but maybe I'll see you later tonight. OK?

SHOEMAKER
OK! Bye, bye.

*(*CARSWELL *exits.)*

MRS. GREENE
(To **MRS. FUTRELL.***)* Tell me if you see Carswell coming back.

*(***MRS. FUTRELL** *walks over and stands by the table at stage left, watching out for* **CARSWELL.***)*

MRS. GREENE
(To **SHOEMAKER.***)* Let me warn you about that man you talked with. He's an ABC card peddler.

SHOEMAKER
Really?

MRS. GREENE
Avoid him, or you'll get yourself in a mess. Be careful!

JACKSON
(Interrupting.) I saw you talk with that man. He's an ABC card peddler. You shouldn't have talked with him.

MRS. FUTRELL
(Waves at **MRS. GREENE** *and* **EVELYN JACKSON** *to signal* **CARSWELL'S** *return.)* Hey, you! Be quiet!

*(***MRS. GREENE** *and* **MISS JACKSON** *pause to think of something else to say next.)*

MRS. FUTRELL
Oops! I goofed. I thought he was coming. Sorry. *(Continues looking.)*

SHOEMAKER
(Looking at **MRS. GREENE,** *still not aware of what is going on around her. Then she looks at* **EVELYN JACKSON.***)* What's wrong with him? He's so nice and so well dressed.

JACKSON

Yes, with his ill-gotten money. Can't you understand? He's going to take advantage of you.

SHOEMAKER

Me? How can he take advantage of me when he offered me a job that pays $300, more than twice as much as I earn now?

JACKSON

But can't you see what kind of job that will be? He'll make you beg for money, sell ABC cards.

SHOEMAKER

He won't make me do that. He asked me to be his assistant, and that's different. I see nothing wrong with that.

MRS. GREENE

Evelyn is right. That man is going to exploit you.

SHOEMAKER

But I like him! I want to work for him. *(Stands up and moves away from the chair.)*

JACKSON

OK, have it your way. You'll be sorry later. You can do as you like, but remember I warned you. *(EVELYN JACKSON, MRS. GREENE, and MRS. FUTRELL follow SHOEMAKER toward the card table on the platform.)*

GREENE

(To YAKUBSKI.) Can I talk to you now?

YAKUBSKI

What is it?

GREENE

I looked through the bank statement. You never deposited the $150 for food and liquor to pay that bill. Why?

YAKUBSKI

There must be some mistake. Show it to me. *(Examines the document.)* I did deposit it. I'll go to the bank and straighten it out.

GREENE

And what about these unpaid bills? *(Takes out a wad of papers.)* Are they mistakes, too?

YAKUBSKI

Let me see them. *(Looks them over.)* This must be a mix-up. What's the matter? Don't get so excited.

GREENE

Explain this mix-up to me.

YAKUBSKI

Sure. *(To PEOPLE who are beginning to gather around them.)* Get lost. This is a private conversation. Leave us alone! None of your business!

GRADY

(To YAKUBSKI.) You sign big. You asked for it. *(Departs.)*

YAKUBSKI

(To GREENE.) Look, this is the wrong place to discuss these things. And it would take too long to explain. Can't you wait until the Board meeting in two weeks?

GREENE

No, I'm the president, and I want to know what's going on.

YAKUBSKI

I tell you, nothing wrong is happening.

(By that time the CROWD *gathers again. Some ask,* "What's wrong?" "Why are they arguing?" *Others answer,* "It's about money.")

GREENE
You can't fool me with your smooth talk. Don't play innocent. I want an explanation now.

YAKUBSKI
What are you trying to insinuate? You have no right to talk that way to me.

GREENE
I have the right, because money is missing, and you are responsible for it.

*(*PEOPLE *repeat,* "Greene says, 'Yakubski stole club money.'")

YAKUBSKI
Yes, I am responsible, but I tell you no money is missing. I'll explain it all at the Board meeting.

GREENE
OK, I'll wait until then. But can you answer one question now?

YAKUBSKI
Go ahead.

GREENE
I understand that you were at the $50 window at the racetrack.

YAKUBSKI
That's just gossip. Maybe it was somebody else who looked like me. *(Pause.)* But what if it were true? What gives you the right to pry into my personal affairs?

GREENE

All right, I'll wait until that meeting. But you better have a good explanation then.

YAKUBSKI

I don't like your attitude. Are you calling me a thief?

GREENE

I'm not calling you anything. I didn't insult you!

YAKUBSKI

But you did! I demand an apology.

GREENE

No. I won't apologize until you prove the money isn't missing.

YAKUBSKI

Are you calling me a thief? *(*YAKUBSKI *approaches* GREENE *with his fists clenched.)*

*(*GRADY *holds him back, while* SHALLECK *holds* GREENE *back.)*

FUTRELL

(To GREENE.*)* Shame on you!

YAKUBSKI

You bastard. You were always jealous of me and plotted against me to be the leader. Now you're gloating. Happy now? I want to smash that ugly mug of yours.

MRS. YAKUBSKI

(Breaks through the CROWD *and pushes* GREENE *in the chest.)* How dare you! You liar! My husband is not a thief.

GREENE

(Pushes **MRS. YAKUBSKI** *aside, and stands up on a chair. To* **MRS. YAKUBSKI.)** Your husband is a thief. *(To the* **CROWD.)** Your treasurer is a thief. He stole the club's money.

YAKUBSKI

(Attempts to approach **GREENE,** *struggling to free himself from people who restrain him.)* Let me go. *(To* **GREENE.)** You got a swelled head! You're crazy! You invented it all, you bastard, to spoil my name. But you'll only spoil your own name! *(To* **MRS. YAKUBSKI.)** Ida, don't believe him. I didn't steal any money.

GREENE

Get out of here, you thief! I'll see you in jail!

YAKUBSKI

You get out! You'll go to jail for blackening my name!

(In the meantime **KLAYMANS** *puts a quarter in the juke box, which lights up with multicolored lights and blares music. As* **GRADY** *turns lights in the room on and off,* **KLAYMANS** *climbs on the platform and waves her hands to attract attention.)*

KLAYMANS

The dance is on. Stop! Shut up! You deafies! Can't you hear? Oh, come on, let's dance! *(To* **LINDSEY, CARSWELL,** *and* **FUTRELL.)** You all move the tables aside! Can't you see the music's started? Let's dance! Let's dance! *(She wiggles her hips.)*

(The tables are moved aside and **COUPLES** *form and begin dancing, including* **CARSWELL** *who dances with* **SHOEMAKER,** *and* **LINDSEY** *who dances with* **KLAYMANS.** *The* **PARIAH** *stands uncertainly in the middle of the dancing* **CROWD.)**

End of Act Two

ACT THREE

Setting as in Act One. Time: two weeks since Act One. Seventeen chairs lie stacked on the platform. **SHALLECK** sweeps the floor.

SHALLECK
(To **HIMSELF**.) They think I'm dumb, but really I'm smart. (Continues to sweep the floor.) Cut it out! (Sweeps some more.) The club depends on me. It's true. Everyone loves me. (Noticing **MRS. FUTRELL** approach him from the restroom stage right, **SHALLECK** stops talking and sweeps faster.)

(**MRS. FUTRELL** then sits down on a bar stool. **GREENE**, **GRADY**, and **KLAYMANS** rush in from the office stage left and set up four chairs. **SHALLECK** becomes annoyed, dropping the broom on the floor, and tells them to go away. **GREENE** exits stage left. **KLAYMANS** and **GRADY** exit stage right. **MRS. FUTRELL** watches **KLAYMANS** exit and walks slowly toward **SHALLECK** who continues sweeping.)

MRS. FUTRELL
(To **SHALLECK**.) You see that? Klaymans is here without her college lover.

SHALLECK
Is that so?

MRS. FUTRELL
I'm not surprised. You know what happened?

SHALLECK
No. What happened?

MRS. FUTRELL

But I don't really want to talk about that woman. Enough is enough.

SHALLECK

Now you've made me curious. Please tell me.

MRS. FUTRELL

You won't tell anyone?

SHALLECK

Cross my heart. My mouth will be zipped up.

MRS. FUTRELL

The college boy rejected her because she's frigid.

SHALLECK

I can't believe that. I know better.

MRS. FUTRELL

That's what someone told me. By the way, did you hear what happened to Yakubski?

SHALLECK

No, tell me!

MRS. FUTRELL

He came to Grady's home last Thursday to play poker, but Grady shut the door in his face.

SHALLECK

Yes, I know. I was there. No, Grady wasn't that rough. He only lied that the game was cancelled, but still he hurt Yakubski plenty.

MRS. FUTRELL
Oh, how gossip spreads! Anyhow, that thief should go to jail for
stealing our money.

SHALLECK
(Drops the broom.) Let the Board decide that. *(Picks it up.)*

MRS. FUTRELL
I sure will be relieved to see him in jail.

SHALLECK
Why? You look so happy about that!

MRS. FUTRELL
Because that hypocrite and his wife will be punished. Hah! Some
people are even saying that Yakubski left town. I'm sure he won't
come here tonight. He won't dare show his face before honest
people. *(Seeing* YAKUBSKI *and* MRS. YAKUBSKI *enter, she stops
talking.)*

*(*YAKUBSKI *and* MRS. YAKUBSKI *wave greetings from the entrance.*
MRS. FUTRELL, *head high, stalks away as the* YAKUBSKIS *look at
each other, surprised, and then watch* MRS. FUTRELL'S *retreating
figure.* MRS. FUTRELL *sets up two more chairs to keep occupied.)*

YAKUBSKI
(To SHALLECK.*)* Hi! Time for me to start selling the tickets.

SHALLECK
Hi!

*(*YAKUBSKI *turns stage left.* MRS. YAKUBSKI *follows him.)*

MRS. YAKUBSKI
(To YAKUBSKI.*)* Don't be upset by that evil woman.

YAKUBSKI
I'm not upset. Relax.

MRS. YAKUBSKI
You relax, too. Everything will be all right. I'm sure the Board will clear your name.

YAKUBSKI
What if that doesn't happen?

MRS. YAKUBSKI
It must happen! You're innocent! I'm going to bawl that woman out.

YAKUBSKI
Don't bother.

MRS. YAKUBSKI
Oh no! She must learn her lesson. *(Goes in search of* MRS. FUTRELL, *finds her.* YAKUBSKI *tries to stop her, and* MRS. YAKUBSKI *shrugs and reluctantly gives in. But when* YAKUBSKI *exits,* MRS. YAKUBSKI *sneaks back to* MRS. FUTRELL.*)*

MRS. YAKUBSKI
(To MRS. FUTRELL.*)* What's going on? Why did you ignore me?

MRS. FUTRELL
Well . . . well . . . oh, I didn't see you.

MRS. YAKUBSKI
Face to face with me, you didn't see me! And only recently you and your husband were begging my husband to help you. That's gratitude!

MRS. FUTRELL
I really don't know what you're talking about. Let me go.

MRS. YAKUBSKI
All right, go! And don't let me see you again.

MRS. FUTRELL
(*To* **FUTRELL** *as he enters from stage right.*) Did you see? Yakubski's wife pestered me. And you, coward! As usual you did nothing.

FUTRELL
What did you expect me to do? I don't fight with women.

MRS. FUTRELL
Nor with men either, you nincompoop. Remember you must be sure to vote against that thief Yakubski!

FUTRELL
I'll do what's right, what's good for the club.

MRS. FUTRELL
How can you be so stubborn? I'm disappointed in you.

FUTRELL
Will you stop pushing me around all the time? I've had it! If I knew what a bitch you can be I never would have married you.

MRS. FUTRELL
What's that?!!! Oh, my heart. (*Clutches her bosom.*) My heart!

FUTRELL
(*Embarrassed.*) Don't try that now!

MRS. FUTRELL
You mean thing. You'll kill me. You know the doctor said that aggravation is bad for my heart.

FUTRELL
That's what you keep telling me.

MRS. FUTRELL
(Moves toward center stage; then to the bar and between two rows of chairs as FUTRELL *follows her.)* You call me a liar! I'll TTY my mother tomorrow and . . .

FUTRELL
(Interrupting.) Look—forget it. Forgive me. I didn't mean . . . I'm sorry.

MRS. FUTRELL
(Stops and turns around to face FUTRELL *closer.)* You're sorry? (FUTRELL *nods.* MRS. FUTRELL *moves forward as* FUTRELL *walks backwards.)* Sorry! Sorry! You'll be sorry when I'm gone, and you have to cook for yourself, wash your filthy clothes yourself.

FUTRELL
OK—OK—

MRS. FUTRELL
Will you vote against that thief Yakubski?

FUTRELL
Well . . . I . . .

*(*YAKUBSKI *enters first to move the table and sets it next to the entrance; then exits. Then* GREENE *enters from the office, stage left.)*

GREENE
(Interrupts FUTRELL.*)* Look, Yakubski has no right to sell tickets for the club. Go tell him that, now!

FUTRELL
Why me? Do it yourself!

GREENE

I can't. Yakubski will think it's personal after the fight we had two weeks ago! I want to keep everything—all relations between Yakubski and me—impersonal. Just club business, that's all. You're a Board member. You'll have to do it for the sake of the club.

FUTRELL

Oh, OK. I'll do it for the club.

GREENE

Well, hurry up.

(**YAKUBSKI** *enters from stage left, carrying a roll of tickets and a cash box.* **GREENE** *and* **MRS. FUTRELL** *move away from them to set up four more chairs.*)

FUTRELL

(*Approaches* **YAKUBSKI**.) What are you doing?

YAKUBSKI

Can't you see? I'm selling tickets for tonight. It's Skit Night.

FUTRELL

I must tell you: you can't do that because you are under suspicion of embezzling the club's money.

YAKUBSKI

What gives you the right to speak to me like that?

FUTRELL

I'm a Board member, right?

YAKUBSKI

And I'm the treasurer! And the By-Laws say I will remain treasurer until the Board decides otherwise.

FUTRELL
(To GREENE.*)* I can't make Yakubski stop.

GREENE
(To FUTRELL.*)* Can't you ever do anything right? Let me take over! Damn it! *(To* YAKUBSKI.*)* You can't sell or handle any money. Give everything to Futrell!

(At the same time MACHER *enters from stage left and watches both men,* GREENE *and* YAKUBSKI.*)*

YAKUBSKI
No, I won't! I'm the legally elected treasurer, and the By-Laws say this is one of my duties.

GREENE
Don't hide behind the By-Laws!

YAKUBSKI
Why not give up your job? I've as much right to mine as you do to yours!

GREENE
No, you don't. Under Section 4, Paragraph 2, of the By-Laws, as club president, I can declare an emergency and order you to stop selling the tickets.

YAKUBSKI
(Sitting down on the table.) Just try and order me!

SHALLECK
Greene is right. He's the president. You have to do as he says.

MACHER
By refusing, you only make things worse for yourself. I promise you a fair decision by the Board. *(Turning to* GREENE.*)* Isn't that true?

GREENE
That's true!

YAKUBSKI
OK, but I want you to know I'm doing this under protest! *(He pushes the roll of tickets and the cash box at* GREENE, *pushes the chair toward stage front, and exits where the coffee urn is located.)*

GREENE
(To FUTRELL.*)* You take over. *(To* MACHER.*)* Pick up the chair and put it back where it belongs.

(As FUTRELL *sits down,* BRANNON *enters the club.)*

FUTRELL
(To BRANNON.*)* That will be four dollars.

BRANNON
Thank you.

GREENE
(To BRANNON.*)* You here again?

BRANNON
Yes. Well, I decided to join the club.

GREENE
Changed your mind again?

BRANNON
Believe me, I mean it this time.

GREENE
You better mean it!

BRANNON
Thank you.

GREENE
That's all you can say? OK, but if you change your mind again, this club will be closed to you forever.

BRANNON
I understand.

GREENE
I'll give you one last chance. You have to find a member to sponsor your application.

BRANNON
Thanks, I'll find someone. *(She approaches* YAKUBSKI.*)* Hi, I got news for you.

YAKUBSKI
Hi, what is it?

BRANNON
I've decided to join the club after all. Will you be my sponsor?

YAKUBSKI
(In turmoil.) You sure picked the wrong person to ask!

BRANNON
I don't understand . . .

YAKUBSKI
I've lost my status here. That's why. Now I'm a nobody, and I can't help you.

BRANNON
But why? What happened?

YAKUBSKI
Let's skip it. I don't feel like talking about it. *(Turns away to face* SHALLECK. BRANNON *goes off puzzled.)*

SHALLECK
(*To* YAKUBSKI.) For a good dresser like you, you look kind of bad, tonight.

MRS. YAKUBSKI
(*To* SHALLECK.) Poor man! It's because of his troubles.

SHALLECK
I understand.

MRS. YAKUBSKI
Just imagine: at the banquet last Saturday after the MSAD tournament, my husband and I were supposed to sit at the head table, but somebody switched our seats to a table near the door with deafies we never met before. They were nice—but my face was red with shame—what my friends must have thought. They knew we were supposed to sit up with the big shots!

SHALLECK
Sorry to hear about it.

YAKUBSKI
Were you at Grady's poker game last Thursday? Don't deny it!

SHALLECK
Yes, I was there.

YAKUBSKI
That bastard! He lied to me when he said the game was cancelled. Thanks, I just wanted to know.

SHALLECK
What do you expect me to do about it?

YAKUBSKI
Nothing. Now I know who my friends are—and who they aren't.

MRS. YAKUBSKI
(To SHALLECK.*)* Can't you see how you hurt my husband? He always thought so highly of your friendship.

SHALLECK
Friendship is one thing, and club business another.

YAKUBSKI
I've got nothing more to say.

SHALLECK
I just mean that . . .

MRS. YAKUBSKI
(Interrupts SHALLECK.*)* But can't you see that it's all Greene's doing? Greene wants to run the club by himself. So he invented a pretext for ruining my husband's name!

SHALLECK
Let the Board be the judge of that.

MRS. YAKUBSKI
Believe me, my husband is innocent!

SHALLECK
All I can say is that the Board will decide when it looks at the evidence.

YAKUBSKI
I'll be a ruined man if the Board votes against me. Do you want that?

MRS. YAKUBSKI
(To YAKUBSKI.*)* Don't worry! You're innocent! They'll clear your name! *(To* SHALLECK.*)* Help him!

SHALLECK
Stop pressuring me.

YAKUBSKI
(To **MRS. YAKUBSKI.***)* Let him be!

MRS. YAKUBSKI
(To **YAKUBSKI.***)* Cheer up! You can't blame him. He's only trying to be fair.

YAKUBSKI
(To **MRS. YAKUBSKI.***)* If you say so. *(Stands up and turns around. Notices* **EVELYN JACKSON** *who just arrived and bought a ticket.)*

MRS YAKUBSKI
Everything will be all right. I must go now and make some coffee. Be patient!

*(***EVELYN JACKSON,** *seeing* **YAKUBSKI,** *comes toward him and sits down at stage front.)*

JACKSON
Good evening. How've you been?

YAKUBSKI
Rotten. I have a terrible headache.

JACKSON
You look it. You should have stayed home.

YAKUBSKI
Stay home? That would be admitting guilt.

JACKSON
Well, you're innocent. You've nothing to worry about, so why be upset?

YAKUBSKI

(Sits down.) They say different. Do you have proof? That's what they ask me! Proof? But I'm innocent. How can you prove you're innocent?

JACKSON

Is it really as bad as that?

YAKUBSKI

Yes.

JACKSON

Suppose you replaced the missing money. Would that help to solve matters?

YAKUBSKI

Some. Still, the deaf may be forgiving, but they never forget. Oh, what's the use of talking about it? The money's missing, and that's that!

JACKSON

Is there some way I can help?

YAKUBSKI

No way!

JACKSON

You make me feel so useless.

YAKUBSKI

I didn't mean to hurt your feelings. I'm really touched by your offer, and I'm grateful to you all the same. Excuse me now. *(Turns to leave.)*

JACKSON

Just remember, I'll always be around whenever you need help.

YAKUBSKI
Thanks. But what's the use . . . ?

(JACKSON silently watches YAKUBSKI move away. YAKUBSKI is then stopped by LINDSEY. JACKSON sits down.)

LINDSEY
Well, so you are here. I didn't expect you. You must be a real masochist! *(Chuckles.)*

YAKUBSKI
If you think I'm a masochist, then you are a sadist!

LINDSEY
Me? *(Grins.)* I came here for the real life drama, not for the skits. This is going to be an exciting evening.

YAKUBSKI
Exciting at my expense, you mean!

(As YAKUBSKI leaves LINDSEY, JACKSON stands up and sees MRS. GREENE coming from the bathroom to stage right. JACKSON greets and hugs her. MRS. GREENE walks toward the bar. MRS. WISEMAN follows a few minutes later. JACKSON spreads her arms to greet MRS. WISEMAN, but MRS. WISEMAN avoids her and walks away toward the bar. MRS. WISEMAN also ignores MCALLISTER who just bought a ticket and walks toward the bar. MACHER enters.)

MCALLISTER
(To MACHER.) Look, two women walked past me without looking at me. They didn't even say "Hi" to me, as if I were nobody now.

MACHER
Oh, come on. Stop whining. Accept it like a man!

MCALLISTER
I can't stand it. I'm fed up!

MACHER

Of course we're disappointed in you. How could you lose to a crummy team like Dayton?

MCALLISTER

Well, I've told you again and again: I made a mistake and missed the last basket. So! I'm human—not Superman.

MACHER

Superman doesn't drink! What about you? Out with it! Tell me the truth!

MCALLISTER

No, damn it! I wasn't drunk! How can I make you believe me?

MACHER

If you weren't drunk, why did you take only three shots all night? Did you have some money on the game yourself?

MCALLISTER

What are you trying to do? I don't bet on games I play in. That was a cheap shot. You know me better.

MACHER

OK, OK! I believe you. We'll just have to start all over.

MCALLISTER

No, I'm not sure I want to. Before, when I came to the club, everybody would come up to me and shake my hand. Now everybody cuts me dead.

MACHER

That'll change when they see you win the tournament for the club. Be patient!

MCALLISTER

Aw, the hell with the deaf world!

MRS. GREENE
(Interrupts MACHER.*)* Finally, here you are! The first skit will begin any moment now. Are you ready?

MACHER
Sure, I'm ready. Let's go. *(To* MCALLISTER.*)* Take it easy.

*(*MRS. GREENE *grabs* MACHER'S *wrist and pulls him toward the stage right exit.)*

MCALLISTER
(To HIMSELF.*)* Shove it! *(*MCALLISTER *moves near the bar to sit down.)*

*(*CARSWELL *and* SHOEMAKER *enter the club and buy tickets from* FUTRELL. SHOEMAKER *skips excitedly toward the front row.)*

SHOEMAKER
(To CARSWELL.*)* Come over here.

CARSWELL
(To SHOEMAKER.*)* That's too close. Let's move down here.

SHOEMAKER
But I like a seat close to the stage. *(Pause.)* All right! I'll move over there to sit next to you. *(Gets up.)*

*(*CARSWELL *and* SHOEMAKER *sit down;* BRANNON *comes toward* GRADY *from the bar and sits down facing them.)*

BRANNON
(To GRADY.*)* Hi, say, what's wrong with Yakubski?

GRADY
Ah, yes, you'd be the last to know. Well, his name's not worth a damn in this club anymore. They say he stole club funds.

BRANNON
Oh, God!

GRADY
The Board is meeting to decide what to do.

BRANNON
Will he be there to defend himself?

GRADY
They have already questioned him.

BRANNON
I'm always the last to learn what's going on. Say, will you do me a favor?

GRADY
It depends.

BRANNON
I'm applying for membership in the club. Will you sponsor my application?

GRADY
Remember the last time I sponsored you, and then you withdrew your application? You embarrassed me publicly. No, not again.

BRANNON
Please! I mean it. This time I really mean it.

GRADY
OK, but remember, don't change your mind again, or my name will be ruined here.

(**MRS. GREENE** *appears on the platform as the Mistress of Ceremonies. She waves to attract* **EVERYONE'S** *attention, until* **EVERY-**

ONE *is seated.* KLAYMANS *moves away from* LINDSEY, *toward the front row of chairs from the back row.* KLAYMANS *"gives the finger" to* LINDSEY *in order to embarrass him, and sits down.)*

MRS. GREENE

Hi folks! Our club's acting company is about to bring you skits, to make you cry with laughter and laugh with tears in your eyes. The first skit will be performed by Grady. It will be about a boy and a girl in a park.

*(*MACHER *enters, carrying two chairs and* MRS. GREENE *exits.)*

MACHER

(To the AUDIENCE *on stage.)* Sorry! I'm not Grady. Be patient! *(*MACHER *places the chairs on the platform. Hollers at* GRADY *two times with his hand cupped around his mouth, but there's no response.)* Oh! I forgot. He's deaf. *(Rushes out to call him. The audience roars with laughter.)*

*(*GRADY *enters and sits down at one end of a bench, panting at some stirring sight, then jumps to the other end, where he mimes an imaginary woman. He moves back to the original end and acts like a man who is smitten by the woman and, move after move, approaches the woman, ogling at her and simpering. Just as he is about to touch the woman, he gets up and mimes the woman getting up and leaving, so that, as he imagines himself to be placing an arm around her shoulders, he embraces the air, and falls to the ground, looking at her with disappointment.* GRADY *bows to the* AUDIENCE *twice. End of first skit. The* AUDIENCE *claps halfheartedly.* MRS. GREENE *comes onto the stage and claps her hands.)*

MRS. GREENE

Thank you, thank you. In the next skit, Mrs. Wiseman will offer a signed rendering of "You Light Up My Life."

(MRS. WISEMAN gets on stage, bumps into the chairs left there, and complains to MRS. GREENE. MRS. GREENE orders MACHER to remove the chairs. They leave her alone on the stage and she, acting somewhat tipsy, offers a fairly incomplete performance of the song while MRS. GREENE from a first row seat, attempts to help her remember the lines. MRS. WISEMAN becomes confused when LINDSEY is talking in the back. She points at him, angrily. Almost EVERYONE looks at LINDSEY, and then back at MRS. WISEMAN. MRS. GREENE tries to prompt MRS. WISEMAN again. The AUDIENCE dig elbows into each other's sides and laugh. Finally MRS. WISEMAN is finished and bows and is helped off stage by MRS. GREENE.)

MRS. GREENE
Wonderful! She memorized it in just two weeks. *(Applauds her.)* But the next skit will be really something. You'll split your sides with laughter. Just wait. First there will be ten minutes intermission. Move around, go get a drink, or relax. Come back on time! Please, don't waste our time. Deaf people like to drag on intermission, yakking. You all know that. *(To KLAYMANS.)* Hurry, get your costume changed. Where are you going?

KLAYMANS
(To MRS. GREENE.) I forgot my suitcase over there. Be right back.

MRS. GREENE
OK, but hurry up, please. *(MRS. GREENE folds her arms waiting.)*

KLAYMANS
Don't worry. *(As she walks past the AUDIENCE on stage, LINDSEY stops her.)*

LINDSEY
Well, where were you last Saturday? We had a date, remember?

KLAYMANS
My aunt came to visit me, and I had no way to let you know.

LINDSEY
How about tomorrow? Are you free then?

KLAYMANS
Sorry, I'm meeting a friend.

LINDSEY
Is he male?

KLAYMANS
Yes.

LINDSEY
That's how it is! Now I see—You stood me up last Saturday on purpose!

KLAYMANS
Not on purpose! It just happened that way. My aunt popped in unexpectedly.

LINDSEY
I don't believe you.

KLAYMANS
Suit yourself. Excuse me. I've got other things to do.

LINDSEY
(Grabs her right arm.) You bitch!

SHALLECK
(Gets up, approaches LINDSEY.*)* Don't say that! Not to her!

LINDSEY
Why butt in?

SHALLECK
It's you who's butting in. You—with your college degree—think you're so smart—but you don't know how to talk to a lady.

LINDSEY
(To **SHALLECK.***)* Lady? I have news for you, friend! She's a cock tease, that's all!

*(***KLAYMANS*** is startled by* **LINDSEY'S** *remark.)*

SHALLECK
That's enough from you. Tell the lady you're sorry, or . . .

LINDSEY
What's it to you? No one asked you to intrude.

SHALLECK
Another big word. I'd like to make you eat your fancy words. Apologize to the lady, or I'll knock your teeth out!

KLAYMANS
(Dashes to stage left to get **GREENE.** *To* **GREENE.***)* Lindsey is insulting me. Please do something!

LINDSEY
(To **GREENE.***)* Get this gorilla away from me! Do something!

GREENE
(To **LINDSEY.***)* I won't permit female club members to be insulted by outsiders. Get out!

LINDSEY
But . . .

GREENE
You've got no right to bully and insult ladies!

LINDSEY

This is between me and the lady. None of your business.

GREENE

But it is our business! We look out for each other! You have a college degree—big deal! You're no better than any of us. We're sincere. We really care for each other. And our manners are a helluva lot better than yours! We have hearts! All you have inside you is a knife and smart aleck words!

SHALLECK

(To LINDSEY.*)* Are you man enough to apologize to the lady?

GREENE

(To LINDSEY.*)* Either apologize or get out!

LINDSEY

(To GREEN *and* SHALLECK.*)* You leave me with no other choice . . . I guess I proved who's dumb.

SHALLECK

(Menacingly.) Who's dumb?

LINDSEY

Me! *(Turning to* KLAYMANS.*)* How do you want me to apologize, lovely lady? Kiss your feet? Say I'm sorry 25 times with my left hand and 25 times with my right? Or buy you a drink?

KLAYMANS

I accept the drink, but only if you really mean you're sorry!

LINDSEY

I do!

KLAYMANS

OK, OK, later. I have to go now. *(Exits stage left.)*

GREENE
(Beckons to **SHALLECK, FUTRELL,** *and* **COLLINS.***)* Time for the Board meeting. Hurry! *(All four exit right.)*

MRS. YAKUBSKI
(To **YAKUBSKI.***)* The Board is meeting now. Will you know as soon as it's over?

YAKUBSKI
I've got no idea.

MRS. YAKUBSKI
I must serve the coffee now. Poor dear, cheer up! Soon it will be over.

YAKUBSKI
I know.

*(***MRS. YAKUBSKI** *goes to kitchen area.* **KLAYMANS** *enters, carrying a small suitcase and sees* **YAKUBSKI.***)*

KLAYMANS
(To **YAKUBSKI.***)* You've always been honest with me. Tell me the truth.

YAKUBSKI
What's there to say?

KLAYMANS
I know you very well. Better than you know yourself. Don't deny it. Tell me the truth. Look, we've always been honest with one another. Did you take that money?

YAKUBSKI
Why would you think I took that money, if I did?

KLAYMANS
I know why. Your son needed it.

YAKUBSKI
(After long hesitation.) Yes. *(Pauses.)* I was stuck. He was out of his mind because of his need for drugs. He said he would rob and kill someone to get money unless I gave him some. I was broke, so . . . *(Shrugs.)*

KLAYMANS
The Board is going to expel you from the club. You better confess!

YAKUBSKI
No! Never!

KLAYMANS
There's no other way! How else can you live with yourself?

YAKUBSKI
What about you and me? How can I live with myself when I always lie to my wife about us?

KLAYMANS
I've told you many times that I'd never marry you and break your wife's heart. Don't change the subject. Confess, and I'm sure the club will forgive you.

YAKUBSKI
I can't! I'm afraid of Green. He's so vindictive. He will see to it that I lose my membership in the club, and you know what that means to me. It's Greene that I'm really afraid of.

(**MRS. GREENE** *rushes toward* **KLAYMANS**.)

MRS. GREENE

The show's on. Hurry up! (**KLAYMANS** *and* **MRS. GREENE** *exit to stage right.* **MRS. GREENE** *then gets on the platform. To* **EVERYONE.**) Folks, the show will start now. Please be seated. Hurry! Don't waste time! Now you will see an exciting and beautiful play, "A Night in Chinatown," enacted by the whole cast. (**MRS. GREENE** *exits.*)

(**KLAYMANS** *enters. She starts packing a suitcase. Enter* **GRADY** *dressed as a Chinese mandarin.*)

GRADY

What are you doing?

KLAYMANS

I'm leaving.

GRADY

Why?

KLAYMANS

I won't tell you.

GRADY

Is there someone else?

KLAYMANS

Yes.

GRADY

You ingrate! I found you in the gutter, brought you here. I gave you a home, food, clothes! Now you want to leave me!

KLAYMANS

Please try to understand. It's my life. I want my freedom. You've been kind to me, but my heart belongs to that American soldier. Please let me go!

GRADY

I'll never let you go! I'll kill you first! *(He chokes her. She falls. He stabs himself with a trick dagger and falls.)*

*(*MACHER *appears from stage right. He is wearing a safari suit and a film director's beret.)*

MACHER

(To GRADY *and* KLAYMANS.*)* Get up! Get up! That won't do! It's awful. It looks so phoney. *(To* GRADY.*)* Choke her with more feeling. Kill her with all your strength. Choke her slowly with anger on your face. *(They are about to start all over.)* Cut! *(*MRS. WISEMAN *gets onto the platform.)*

KLAYMANS

. . . my heart belongs to that American soldier. Please let me go!

GRADY

I'll never let you go. I'll kill you first. *(Re-enacts choking in accordance with* MACHER'S *instructions. Then he stabs himself and falls beside* KLAYMANS.*)*

MACHER

(Enters.) That's much better. *(To* GRADY.*)* You've improved. *(Points at* KLAYMANS' *body.)* It looks so true to life. I'm proud of you. You'll win an Oscar. *(To* KLAYMANS.*)* Hey, you, get up! *(Kneels at her side, shakes her.)* Something's wrong.

MRS. GREENE *and* **MRS. WISEMAN**

(Rush on stage.) Call the ambulance! Call the police!

MACHER

(To GRADY.*)* What have you done!

MRS. FUTRELL *and* **JACKSON**

(Spring up and several others react hysterically.) Call the police! Call the ambulance!

(MRS. GREENE and MRS. WISEMAN rush off stage.)

GRADY
(To MACHER.) I didn't know my own strength.

(KLAYMANS gets up. GRADY and MACHER are paralyzed with shock.)

KLAYMANS
Why are you so upset?

GRADY and MACHER
(Together.) We thought you were dead! *(Collapsing.)*

(KLAYMANS, GRADY and MACHER, with drunken MRS. WISEMAN standing in front of them all, bow before EVERYONE. AUDIENCE on stage claps wildly.)

(GREENE, SHALLECK, FUTRELL, COLLINS enter. FUTRELL gets up from the chair and motions to SHALLECK. BOTH walk to front right of center stage.)

YAKUBSKI
(To SHALLECK.) What did the Board decide?

SHALLECK
(Whispers to YAKUBSKI.) The vote was against you. You're expelled from the club.

YAKUBSKI
Expelled from the club?

SHALLECK
Yes, expelled from the club.

YAKUBSKI

I knew it! I knew it! But still . . . I can't believe it. . . . I can't believe it. . . . *(He sits down heavily.)*

(All BOARD *members gather at the bar. The news of the* BOARD'S *decision spreads. People sign together furtively about* YAKUBSKI. FUTRELL *brings the projector to the table.)*

GRADY

(To his neighbors.) Yakubski was expelled from the club!

CARSWELL

(To SHOEMAKER *and* BRANNON.*)* They expelled Yakubski!

MRS. GREENE

(To EVERYONE.*)* We saved the best for last. Our next skit is called "The Operating Room." I've got a bottle of smelling salts in my purse for any man, woman, or child who faints. People sensitive to the sight and smell of blood are advised to close their eyes during this skit.

*(*MRS. GREENE *and* MRS. WISEMAN *carry on two sawhorses and set them up.* GRADY *and* MACHER *enter wearing surgical outfits and carrying* KLAYMANS *on a board covered up with a white sheet; only her head is visible. The board is laid on the two sawhorses.* MRS. WISEMAN *is also in a surgical outfit and assisting as a nurse.)*

FIRST DOCTOR

(To NURSE.*)* Pass me the scapel.

NURSE

(To FIRST DOCTOR.*)* I don't know what it is.

SECOND DOCTOR

(To FIRST DOCTOR.*)* You spelled the word wrong. S-C-A-L-P-E-L.

FIRST DOCTOR
(To SECOND DOCTOR.*)* Oh! *(To* NURSE.*)* Scalpel!

NURSE
(Looking around for it. To FIRST DOCTOR.*)* I still don't know what it looks like.

*(*FIRST DOCTOR *describes it in gestures.)*

NURSE
Oh, that! OK! *(Picks up imaginary knife and hands to* FIRST DOCTOR.*)*[15]

*(*FIRST DOCTOR *proceeds to cut the patient, who is kicking and screaming, and moving her head.)*

SECOND DOCTOR
(To FIRST DOCTOR.*)* Oh, God! We forgot to put her to sleep. *(He mimes giving the* PATIENT *a mask to cover face and turning on the ether.* PATIENT *grows quiet.)*

*(*FIRST DOCTOR *makes a ripping, slicing motion, then plunges his arm into* PATIENT'S *stomach, searches and extricates a hearing aid which he lifts high for all to see, and whose function he mimes.)*

FIRST DOCTOR
What's that? A hearing aid?[16]

NURSE
The patient is deaf.

FIRST DOCTOR
And dumb! She swallowed it, thinking it would help her hear. *(Laughs. Puts hearing aid into* NURSE'S *hands.)*

(FIRST DOCTOR then draws out in succession a microphone, a portable radio, and a loudspeaker, all of which he displays to the AUDIENCE. He then hands one after another to the NURSE.)

SECOND DOCTOR
Look! *(He plunges his hand into the PATIENT's body and draws out a tongue.)* She's an oralist. She used that tongue to learn how to babble. And here's more . . . *(Draws out a book.)* Look, an English textbook. She's a real brainwashed oralist. OK, I think that's all.

FIRST DOCTOR
Let me see. *(FIRST DOCTOR plunges his arm deeply into the opened stomach, and a hand which is really SECOND DOCTOR's hand appears out of PATIENT's mouth. SECOND DOCTOR bites the hand and FIRST DOCTOR withdraws his arm/hand with a scream.)*

FIRST DOCTOR
Ouch! OK, that's all. Finished. No more. *(To NURSE.)* Give me a needle and thread. The green thread.

SECOND DOCTOR
(To FIRST DOCTOR.) Pink is better. It matches her skin color.

FIRST DOCTOR
OK. Go and get it. Hold it! Now that her belly is empty, we have to put something back inside it. What?

NURSE
A TTY?

FIRST DOCTOR
Yeah! That's great. *(Inserts it into PATIENT's stomach.)*

SECOND DOCTOR
I got an idea! A T-shirt with ABC's in sign on the front! *(Inserts it.)*

FIRST DOCTOR
Here's a book on ASL! ASL is our language. *(Inserts it.)* Is that all we have to put inside her?

SECOND DOCTOR
One more thing we almost forgot. An "I Love You" button.[17] *(Inserts it.)*

*(**BOTH DOCTORS** exchange glances and agree that this is all. **NURSE** gives needle and thread to **FIRST DOCTOR**, and he sews up the wound with big spiral motions. He asks **NURSE** for scissors, and when **NURSE** is slow, he bites off the thread himself. When **SECOND DOCTOR** removes mask from face, **PATIENT** springs up and raises her arm in Deaf Power salute.)*

MRS. GREENE
*(To **EVERYONE**.)* Come on. Applaud them. *(**EVERYONE** claps wildly.)*

*(**MRS. GREENE** calls directly to the four **ACTORS** to come to the platform. All bow before the **AUDIENCE**, including **MRS. WISEMAN** who awkwardly moves in front of the others to bow.)*

MRS. GREENE
More! More! *(**EVERYONE** continues to applaud.)* That's all folks! Next show is in the fall. The bar is open now. And don't forget! A captioned movie will start in 15 minutes. We'll sell sandwiches and coffee now. Help yourself and enjoy!

MRS. YAKUBSKI
*(To **YAKUBSKI**.)* What happened? What did the Board decide? *(**YAKUBSKI** doesn't answer.)* You stand here like a stone! For God's sake, tell me!

YAKUBSKI
The Board voted to expel me from the club.

MRS. YAKUBSKI
It's that Greene! *(She rushes toward* MRS. GREENE. YAKUBSKI *tries to stop her, but she pushes him away. To* MRS. GREENE.*)* It was your husband who stole the money, not my husband. You should be ashamed of yourself!

MRS. GREENE
Leave me alone. Are you crazy? *(*MRS. GREENE *moves away.* MRS. YAKUBSKI *grabs her left arm, but* MRS. GREENE *pulls it away and walks away from her.)*

MRS. YAKUBSKI
If I'm crazy, then you are sly. You fox. You and your husband plotted all this yourselves.

MRS. GREENE
(To EVERYONE.*)* Help! Look, what should I do? She's out of her mind!

MRS. YAKUBSKI
Liar! Hypocrite!

MRS. GREENE
Your husband is a thief! *(*MRS. GREENE *runs toward* MR. GREENE.*)*

MRS. YAKUBSKI
(To YAKUBSKI.*)* Let's leave. They ganged up against you. We're not wanted here. Let's go and never come back!

YAKUBSKI
OK!

MRS. YAKUBSKI
Let me just give the coffee money to Shalleck and settle accounts with him. Then we're finished. Back in a moment.

YAKUBSKI
All right!

(EVERYONE'S eyes are on YAKUBSKI when he walks toward SPIVEY, who is standing alone.)

YAKUBSKI
(To SPIVEY.) You look as if you understood what's happening to me. But you don't really care. Do you? That deathly grin of yours . . . The fires of hell are beckoning to me in your eyes. You don't answer? Of course, you won't. Well, now I feel like I've crossed over to your side. We're brothers now: both outcasts. How low I've fallen! *(He climbs the dais as EVERYONE stares at him. Slowly, as if struggling to carve out each phrase.)* Look! I admit I stole the club's money. But it wasn't for myself. It was for my son. He needed a fix, and he was desperate. He threatened to do anything—rob or kill—to get that money. That was why I went to the racetrack. I hoped to replace the missing money by betting, but I only lost more money and sank deeper into debt. So now I'm expelled from the club? OK, I deserve it. I don't know why I didn't admit it sooner when Greene first approached me about it. I guess I was afraid. To be kicked out of the club is the worst punishment you can give any deaf person. *(With increasing violence.)* Where can I go? What will I do? Stay at home? Home is lonely with only my wife. Home is nothing. The club is my real home, my first home. I live for the club. Punish me in any other way, if you like, but why kick me out? *(He waits for some kind of response from someone, but nobody says anything. He stumbles drunkenly. To GREENE.)* Now, are you satisfied?

MRS. YAKUBSKI
(Approaches YAKUBSKI.) So you did steal the money?

YAKUBSKI
(Nods his head.) Yes. I'm leaving. Are you coming along?

(As they exit, YAKUBSKI *stops, takes from his pocket the birthday pen given him by the club and hands it to* SPIVEY.*)*

(There is a moment of silence. Then EVERYONE *talks at once until* COLLINS *attracts their attention by waving his hands.)*

COLLINS
(To GREENE.*)* But I don't understand. We deaf people accept Carswell who deliberately takes money from people, but you reject Yakubski who took money from us only because he couldn't help it.

SHALLECK
No use arguing about that. Carswell takes money from the hearies. Yakubski took our own money from the club.

CARSWELL
(To COLLINS.*)* You accuse *me* of stealing money? Who, me? No, you're wrong. I'm only taking back what hearing people took from me because I'm deaf.

McALLISTER
But Yakubski himself is deaf! Before, I was somebody. Now, I'm a nobody, because I lost a game. Before, Yakubski was somebody. Now, he's nothing, like me, just because, like me, he made a mistake and lost the game. I'm an Indian, but I'm deaf first. So that's how you treat the deaf! Why be so hard on Yakubski? Why can't we just suspend him?

LINDSEY
(To McALLISTER.*)* I agree with you. I feel different tonight. I think a suspension is reasonable enough. *(To* GREENE.*)* Is that possible?

GREENE
I don't know.

(Commotion as **EVERYBODY** *starts talking at once. Suddenly lights begin to flash on and off as* **GRADY** *manipulates the light switch.* **GRADY** *leaps on the dais.)*

GRADY
Hey, folks! I can't wait any longer. The movie's starting now. I have to send back the film tomorrow, so hurry up, sit down, get ready! I can't wait all night! *(***GRADY*** turns on the projector.)*

(Lights go out as the pulsating beam of the projector illuminates the gradually subsiding commotion as people cease talking and sit down.)

Curtain

NOTES

1. Linguists have demonstrated a fact that many deaf Americans have known for some time: American Sign Language is a language in its own right, with its own vocabulary (words), syntax (word order), grammar (rules for combining words in ways that make sense), idioms, and so forth. Like other languages, such as Chinese or English, it has various dialects. Just as a speaker of English from Scotland sounds different from a speaker from the United States, or a speaker from Harvard sounds different from a speaker from Ole Miss, signers from various parts of the country or from various backgrounds observe dialect differences among themselves. Since Gallaudet College is the only liberal arts college for the deaf, it attracts students with many different dialects. In Act One, Lindsey asserts that Gallaudet has a homogenizing effect on the language and sets a "national standard." Grady notices that Lindsey's language sets him apart from the others.

2. TTY refers to a variety of electronic devices that enable deaf individuals and those who cannot use their voices to communicate by telephone with others who have a similar device. A TTY or MCM or TDD usually consists of a coupler or transmitter on which the telephone receiver sits, a keyboard for typing in messages, and a display screen or roll of paper for receiving messages.

3. ABC cards, or manual alphabet cards, depict every handshape necessary for fingerspelling along with the corresponding printed letter. (See note 9.)

4. Retinitis pigmentosa (RP) refers to a group of hereditary diseases which cause degeneration of the retina. This degeneration causes serious vision loss. The common symptoms are 1) poor vision in the dark, 2) gradual loss of peripheral (side) vision, and 3) gradual loss of central vision. Usher's Syndrome (US) refers to an inherited condition of deafness or severe hearing impairment plus RP. Ballin, suffering from US, is already deaf, and his loss of peripheral vision has reached the point that his vision is now narrow like a tunnel.

5. There exists a controversy in deaf education between *oralists,* who insist that deaf children should be educated through lipreading and speech therapy to adapt to the hearing world, and *others,* who argue that a purely oral education is not sufficient for all deaf children and that signing or manual communication is a legitimate mode of communication for the deaf. The latter disparagingly refer to an oralist as a hippopotamus—flapping lips— because of the exaggerated lip movements that the oralist must practice. Sometimes the word hippopotamus is applied to hearing people in general.

6. Comité International des Sports des Sourds is a multinational organization that promotes sports among hearing-impaired athletes. CISS organizes world games, sets international standards, maintains international records, and publishes a bilingual newsletter on the results of international competitions.

7. The National Association of the Deaf (NAD), perhaps the oldest national organization of the deaf, has 47 state associations plus local chapters in most cities of the United States. NAD holds annual conventions. The conventions are not only festive social occasions but also opportunities to plan the serious political, educational, and cultural efforts that the NAD carries out. NAD has accomplished many goals, such as securing the right of deaf drivers to be licensed to operate automobiles, lobbying for equitable insurance rates for deaf drivers, demanding adequate counsel for deaf individuals in legal proceedings, and so forth. The initials in the stage directions and in the dialogue are meant to suggest a chapter of NAD.

8. SEE is an acronym for Seeing Essential English and for Signing Exact English. These systems of communication were developed by educators and parents to teach English to hearing-impaired children. Signs from American Sign Language were adapted, and gestures were invented to represent certain features of English (such as the articles "a" and "the," and the verb endings "-ing" and "-ed," and others). Signs are used in English word order, rather than according to American Sign Language grammar. Mr. and Mrs. Greene are living in a bilingual household where they find that their native language, American Sign Language, is influenced by their children's "school language," SEE.

9. Fingerspelling consists of one handshape for each letter of the Roman alphabet. By using fingerspelling, one can represent manually exactly what one would say or write in English, for example. The issue between Lindsey and Grady results from Lindsey's fingerspelling English words—words unfamiliar to Grady, who feels that Lindsey is flaunting his college education and his fluency in English.

10. See note 5.

11. Because many deaf people cannot rely on buzzing doorbells, clanging alarm clocks, or ringing telephones, they often adapt systems of flashing lights to alert them to these objects.

12. Section 504 of the Rehabilitation Act of 1973 prohibits discrimination against disabled people (including those who are hearing-impaired) in jobs, education, and services at agencies or institutions that receive federal funds.

13. Because they cannot hear the language, deaf people face obstacles in acquiring English—obstacles that do not impede hearing people. How well a deaf person uses English is *not at all* a reflection of that person's intelligence, even though many hearing people assume mistakenly that a deaf individual who has difficulty with English must be "dumb." For many hearing-impaired individuals, English may, in fact, be a second or third language.

14. Washoe is a chimpanzee who was raised very much like a human child in the home of two psychologists, Beatrice Gardner and R. Allen Gardner. They taught her to communicate through sign language.

15. The actors are joking about the contrast between *gesture* (which the doctor immediately understands) and *fingerspelling* (which relies on English). For more explanation, see notes 1, 9, and 13.

16. While a hearing aid is often useful to one whose hearing is impaired, some deaf people who cannot benefit at all from such a device resent the assumption of many hearing people that a hearing aid "cures" deafness. Such a mistaken assumption not only overestimates the efficacy of hearing aids; it also implies that deafness is an illness or a defect that one ought to get rid of.

17. One can fingerspell the initial letters, I, L, and Y, simultaneously on one hand. This configuration is often represented on pins, buttons, posters, and so forth as an acceptance of deaf people, their disability, and their unique mode of communication.

This book was typeset in Century Schoolbook by Carver Photocomposition of Arlington, Virginia, and printed and bound by Automated Graphic Systems of White Plains, Maryland. It was designed by Donna Simons.